Thanks to the many Brothers & Sisters whom have given up much love, in appreciation of this message,

"From Niggas To Gods Pt. 1."

May Peace & Blessings
Be Upon You All.

(brief excerpts from a few letters)

"...(A Brother/Teacher) recently allowed me to experience the book, *'From Niggas to Gods Pt. 1.'* You've given the Spirit of Truth a clear, resounding, penetrating, far reaching voice. In producing these writings, you have fashioned an effective tool that can pierce the crust of ignorance that covers the collective Black mind."

-Brother from
The Midwest

"I am writing in regards to your book, *'From Niggas to Gods Pt. 1.'* Your book is well needed in the Black community. It provides enlightenment that we all need, as a Black nation. I really enjoyed it and can't wait for Part II."

-Brother from
The Midwest

"Much peace, love and respect to you sir. I enjoyed reading your book *'From Niggas to Gods Pt. 1.'* I thank you for writing a book of that nature. It enlightened my mind and helped me with my quest, to wake up to reality since I've been incarcerated. I also began to find out about myself and what I like to do in life other than chillin' with the fellas and getting in trouble. I believe that it's time for me to put away my foolish and childish ways. When I get back into society I'm going to make it a must to become a better man than I was before."

-Brother from
The Midwest

"This book is the perfect guide to prepare an African-American with full knowledge of self."

-Brother from
The West Coast

All Praise Be To The Most High
Make way for The Creams of The Planet.
"God Crushed to The Earth, shall Rise Again!!!"

FROM NIGGAS TO GODS

(PART ONE)

International Standard Book Number
#1-56411-064-8

Manufactured in the United States of America
(Self-Help/Spirituality/Black Studies $12.95)

First Printing, December 1993
Second Printing, September 1994
Third Printing, April 1995
Fourth Printing, January 1996
Fifth Printing, July 1996
Sixth Printing, May 1997
Seventh Printing, September 1997
Eighth Printing, April 1998
Ninth Printing, November 1998

Published By:
Nia Communications/Press
P.O. Box 724742 • Atlanta, GA • 31139-1742

Toll-Free Order Line 1-888-244-5770
w h o l e s a l e & r e t a i l b o o k s e l l e r s

Other Books By Author
Currently in Print

---

1. **"There are only Two Religions in the Whole World?"**
   Religious Confusion vs. The Black Spiritual Rise
   Akil (80 pgs. Nia Comm./Press $7.95)

2. 12-Lessons To Restore The Image,
   The Character, & The Responsibility of:
   "The Goddess Blackwoman"
   Akil (170 pgs. Nia Comm./Press $12.95)

3. **"From Niggas to Gods Vol. II"**
   Akil (301pgs. Nia Comm./Press $14.95)

4. **"How to Praise Your God For-Real!"**
   Religious Confusion vs. The Black Spiritual Rise Pt. 2
   Akil (75 pgs. Nia Comm./Press $7.95)

To order send check or money order to: Attn: Nia Comm. Ordering
P.O. Box 724742, Atlanta, GA 31139-1742
Allow 4-6 wks for delivery
Please make payable to Nia Comm./Press
Include $4.00 shipping and handling (add 1.00 per add'l book)

FROM

NIGGAS
TO GODS

PART ONE
BY AKIL

<u>DEDICATION</u>

These writings are dedicated to the 'Gang-Truce', and to those who did not live to see it. It's time-out for all of these 'Crippled-Bloods' and 'Bloody-Crips'. Just like Ice Cube said, "We all just po-niggas, nappy hair and big lips." So, what's the trip???

FROM NIGGAS TO GODS PT. 1

Dedication

Foreword

Introduction

CHAPTERS

Final Word (Outro)

Nuff-Respect To:

<u>FOREWORD</u>

THIS IS A COMPILATION OF INDIVIDUAL ESSAYS WRITTEN DURING THE SUMMER-FALL OF 1992. THE ESSAYS ARE DESIGNED TO INSPIRE THOUGHT WITHIN THE BLACK MIND. THESE WRITINGS ARE PRIMARILY TARGETED TOWARD THE BLACK YOUTH OF THIS DAY, OF WHICH I AM A PART OF. I AM NOT A MASTER OF THESE TEACHINGS, BUT THESE TEACHINGS I WISH TO MASTER.

"THEY" SAY THAT MY GENERATION IS NOT INTELLIGENT ENOUGH TO READ A BOOK. I SAY THAT "THEY" ARE WRONG. IT IS JUST THAT "THEY" ARE NOT WRITING ABOUT ANYTHING OF INTEREST THAT IS RELEVANT TO OUR LIVES!

AND WHEN "THEY" DO WRITE SOMETHING, THEY HAVE TO WRITE IN THE PERFECT "KING'S ENGLISH" TO IMPRESS THEIR HARVARD PROFESSORS! HERE WE ARE WITH A BOOK IN ONE HAND, AND A DICTIONARY IN THE OTHER, TRYING TO UNDERSTAND WHAT IN THE HELL THE AUTHOR IS INTELLECTUALLY MASTURBATING ABOUT!!!

IF YOU HAVE GOT SOMETHING TO SAY, JUST SAY IT! WE ARE NOT IMPRESSED BY YOUR 27-LETTER WORDS, OR YOUR SHAKESPEARIAN STYLE OF WRITING. THE BLACK YOUTH OF TODAY DON'T GIVE A DAMN ABOUT SHAKESPEARE!!! THIS AIN'T NO DAMN POETRY CONTEST! WE ARE DEALING WITH THE SALVATION OF OUR ENTIRE BLACK NATION!

IF YOU WANT TO REACH THE PEOPLE, YOU HAVE TO EMBRACE US WHERE WE ARE, AND THEN TAKE US WHERE WE NEED TO GO. SO THESE WRITINGS ARE <u>FROM</u> MY GENERATION AND <u>FOR</u> MY GENERATION, WITH RESPECT AND LOVE.

IF NO ONE WILL TEACH, LOVE, AND GUIDE US, THEN WE WILL TEACH, LOVE, AND GUIDE OURSELVES.

PEACE,

YOUR BRO. DRE' (AKIL)

INTRODUCTION

So, here we are. Here we are, the Mothers and Fathers of Supreme <u>Civilization</u>, living within the most self-destructive <u>uncivilized</u> state of mind, called "Nigga". "Nigga" is a state of mind that leads to a state of existence. "Nigga" is the state of mind and existence in which we now live. So, here we are.

How did we get here? We have not always lived within this state of mind. We once lived within a state of mind that produced Supreme Black Excellence, and Supreme Black Genius. Our Ancestors called this state of mind and state of existence "God". We were all divine Gods and Goddesses, but children of the most high God, who serves as our Master Teacher toward the divinity within our own nature.

Well as you know, we are no longer existing on the level of "Gods and Goddesses", we are now existing on the level of "Niggas". We have been psychologically, biologically, and therefore spiritually reduced from "Gods to Niggas". We have been destroyed and reduced to dust.

Look, all of this tragedy is true, but wait! Today is a good day! Today is a new day! This is the beginning of our re-construction. The days of our destruction are over. This is the day that we return "From Niggas To Gods"!

We have spent all of our time and energies toward our own <u>self-destruction</u>, but now those same energies will be re-channeled toward our own <u>self-construction</u>.

But wait, wait, wait, wait. We want to negate our course on the path of truth that will lead us out of the lies that have shackled us down for so many centuries. Understand that before we get to where we are going, we have to tell some straight, honest, hard truth about where we are right now.

These writings will not necessarily say anything new. The truth ain't new. The truth is as ancient as time itself. These writings will only tell you the truth in a particular arrangement and language that is clearly understandable for these times.

These writings are not designed to solve the problems of this world. These writings are primarily designed to inspire the thought process. These writings are designed to inspire thought within those young precious Black minds, that will ultimately produce the solutions to the problems of this world.

So, before we make this move back "From Niggas To Gods", let us tell some of this hard, raw, straight-foward, un-compromising, honest-to-God truth, that will qualify us to make this divine ascension.

<u>YOU ARE STILL A SLAVE!!!</u>

Are we still confined to the chains of slavery? Many people believe that the enslavement of Black men, women, and children, is a thing of the past. The world believes that AmeriKKKa has set her black slaves free, from the bondage of their white slavemasters. Even some Black people in AmeriKKKa, believe that they are actually free from the mastery, and control of their white oppressors.

In fact, <u>most</u> Black people in AmeriKKKa today have been psychologically duped into believing that they actually operate according to their own will. These misled perceptions can not be further from the actual truth. You are, <u>indeed</u>, <u>in-thought</u>, and <u>in-fact</u>, still a slave.

Now, wait a minute! I know that many of you are saying, "I don't know what he talking about! Don't nobody tell me what to do and I go where I want to go whenever I want to go!" Well you are right to a certain extent. You can do whatever you want to do and you can go wherever you want to go, but consider this.

You ain't doing nothing and you ain't going nowhere! The slavemasters don't have to chain you down or whip your black ass anymore, because you ain't doing nothing and you ain't going nowhere!!!! You have freedom, in name, but not in definition! You <u>are</u> <u>not</u> a slave in name, but you <u>are</u> in definition!

The definition of the word <u>slave</u> means, "one who is

dominated by some outside influence and having no personal rights or freedom." Now, are you dominated by some outside influence other than your own internal influence? Do you have your personal rights and your true freedom? Do you really know and understand what freedom actually is? Have you ever truly experienced true freedom? Do you even remember what true freedom was all about? What do you know other than what white people have told you? Nothing! What do you know other than what black folks have told you, that they heard from other white folks? Nothing!!!

Yes, the physical slavery is "somewhat" over, but what about the biological slavery? What about the economical slavery? What about the sociological slavery? What about the spiritual slavery? What about the psychological slavery?

The physical chains were just one aspect amidst the many horrors of slavery! The chains are off of our hands, but we ain't producing nothing! The chains are off of our feet, but we ain't going no where! Why? Why? Why?

This is because those physical chains were the least of our worries! We still have the biggest chain of all wrapped around our minds, hearts, and souls! Your mind is still locked-down, and it is your mind that controls your hands and your feet! That's like having a brand new shiny car, but the engine is locked up! Having a car that can't go nowhere is just like not having a car at all!

What are you doing? ...Nothing! Where are you going? ...Nowhere? The whiteman took the chains off our hands and feet because we stopped swinging and we stopped kicking! So why not take the damn chains off?! We had been in the chains for so long, that we had forgotten why the white slavemaster put them on us in the first place! We have forgotten the original reason and purpose for the physical chains! The chains were to hold you down, but if you ain't tryin to get up, then the chains have outlived their purpose! Think about that for a while. Stop reading for a second. I want you to think!

Let us attempt to make this point a bit clearer by using an example. I want you to stay open minded and stop thinking like the slave that you were made to be. Let us use a hypothetical example along with our imaginations.

The relationship between a dog and it's master can be directly paralleled to the relationship between the black people and their white slavemasters, for the past 4 centuries in AmeriKKKa. This is very true! I want you to open your mind, and really think about this objectively. Consider this.

Suppose that tomorrow, for some reason, you became interested in getting a pet dog for your family or household. Suppose that you then go to the pet store to look around, and you find a dog that you are interested in buying. You then purchase the dog and bring it back to your home. Now once you get home you notice that this dog is a bit active and untamed, so you purchase a collar for the dog and chain the dog to a tree in the backyard. Since the dog is untamed, you have to begin training the dog to obey your commands.

You can eventually train this dog to do everything, from catching a frisbee to attacking an enemy of yours, at a single command. But before you train your new dog to do all of these other things, you must first train your dog to not run away from you and to return to you at your immediate command. Right? You have to keep choking the dog with that collar until the dog stops trying to run-away from you.

You also have to give the dog food and water on a daily routine schedule, so that it will become totally dependent upon you for physical and nutritional survival. The dog will forget how to independently hunt and find food for itself, therefore persuading the dog away from any desires to flee away from you or to do for its' self.

Also I must add that anytime the dog does anything to disobey you, you will either whip it, or deny it its scheduled meal or food. Also, anytime the dog is extra obedient to your wishes, you will give the dog extra food and a pat on the head. This psychological training is absolutely necessary to gain total control over your animal (or nigga). You must break down its' free spirit, tame it, and make it totally dependent upon you. This is the only way to win your animal's (or nigga's) obedience,   permanently.

After a while, you will have your dog so obedient, and so well trained, that you can take the collar off the dog, and un-chain the dog from the tree. The dog can now roam freely because you have it so well trained, that it will run to you at your very command! The dog isn't going anywhere! The dog now loves you! The dog loves you because you feed it everyday! It is happy and satisfied to get dog-slop and water everyday, even though you may be in the house eating a full steak-dinner everyday!

The dog believes that it deserves nothing better than dog-slop. The dog is so grateful to you because it remembers those days that you denied it food, for reasons of its' disobedience to you, and the dog has forgotten how to provide for itself, like in the days of its' independence. The dog loves you because it remembers when it was chained to that tree in the backyard, and it also remembers the day that you unchained its' neck from the tree! So the dog licks your hand everytime it remembers that you set it free!!!

But, what the dog has failed to remember, is that you were the same no-good bastard that chained it to the tree in the first place!!! Yes, that dog (nigga) has totally forgotten that you were the one who purchased him. Purchased him from the bondage of one man to be under your bondage. The dog has been psychologically tricked by you. So the dog does not recognize you for who you really are. The dog has forgotten that you are the no-good bastard that originally locked him up!!!

So you had better not let that dog remember that fact! Because as soon as that dog is reminded of that fact, that will be the same day that the dog bites you in your ass!!! That dog will then proceed to bite everybody's ass, in the family that has been smiling at it for all these years! The dog will then leave your house, never to come back again! Do you understand what I'm saying? Do you really understand what is being said to you? Think about it. Really think about it.

Now if your dog (nigga) does leave you one day, how will you handle it? How will you react? Will you react violently and chase the dog? Will you mourn over the fact that your dog has left you? After all, "...dog is man's best friend." You know what they say... "some of my best friends are Blacks...oops! I mean dogs! (...oops I mean niggas!)

If your dog leaves you, will you miss the way it use to curl up around your feet and lick your boots clean? Will you miss the way it use to do anything just to get you to pat its' head? It just loved your attention.

Will you miss the way it use to dance and wag its' tail, for your entertainment? Will you miss the dogs' protection? Will you miss the way it would attack any of your enemies, even if the enemies were other dogs (niggas) that looked just like it! You would not even have to break a sweat. The dog would fight all of your fights for you. Will you miss the loyal service of your well trained dog? I wonder if you will. I really wonder.

I also wonder will whitefolks miss us so-called negroes once we get smart enough to leave them! I wonder will we ever start to remember how we got here in the first place! I wonder if we will start remembering who put the chains on us in the first place, and will we ever realize why they took them off!!!

They did not take the chains off of us because they felt ashamed of the horrible crimes they committed against us!!! Don't be a fool to believe that! They took the chains off, because us negroes were so psychologically trained, that we were not going anywhere anyway!!! This is the truth!

So now we live our entire lives running around his backyard, doing what we have been trained to do and hoping for an extra dog biscuit, a pat on the head, or some left over scraps from the slavemasters table! Yes, this is the absolute truth! This is the truth and don't try to deny it! Because the first loyalty of a dog (nigga) to its' master, is to protect its' master!!! So stop barking slave, cause you barking up the wrong tree!!! Stop barking and face the truth!!! You are still nothing but the whiteman's nigga!!!

I know that the truth hurts, but you must understand that you and I have been psychologically duped! We have been deceived! We have been misled! We have just plain been lied to! You must understand and know this, because knowing is half the battle! The other half of the battle is fighting what you now know is wrong! But how are you going to fight a problem if you don't even know what the problem is? Now let's look at this thing, so that we will know what the problem is ! Let us try to calm our personal emotions, and just think objectively.

Yes, you are still a slave. A slave is something or someone, who is not in control of his or her own thoughts and actions. Do you understand what that means? This means that a slave has absolutely no control over themselves, and I just said that you are indeed, in thought, and in fact still a slave! That is serious.

Your thoughts and your actions make-up the basis upon which your entire life is built. Your thoughts and actions are the only two things that you can actually call your own! Those are the only two things that are truly yours! Not your money! Not your car! Not your house! Not your clothes! Not your furniture! Not your television! Not your stereo! Not your girlfriend! Not your boyfriend! Not your husband! Not your wife! Not your child!

None of this can be called your own, because you came into this world without it, and you are going to leave this world without it! So, you really can't even claim your own Black ass, because you can't even take your body with you when you leave this earth!!! The molecules and atoms that bond together to form and make up your rusty Black-butt, must return back to the soil of the earth, where it came from in the first place! Think about it!

Now, do you understand what I am saying, when I say that all that you actually have in life, are your thoughts and your actions? Well Blackman and Blackwoman, you don't even have that! You are not even in control of your thoughts and actions! You are just like that dog!

Your whole entire life is centered around the way that this slavemaster has trained you! Yes, it's true! I have no reason to lie to you because I'm right down in hell with you! The only difference between me and you, is that I know that we are in hell and you don't!

I know that real devil who put us in hell and you don't! I'm running around trying to get the hell out of hell, while you running around begging the devil for a cool glass of water, and scratching your head wondering why it is so damn hot in here. You running all around, hot as hell, while the devil is just coolin-out trying to get a sun tan! He don't feel the heat because he is right at home! He is as comfortable as can be, just laughing at your black ass! Just laughing at my black-ass!!!

All of your thoughts and actions are directly or indirectly controlled by the psychological training of the slavemaster. We are just like that loyal dog. Our thoughts and actions are not ours anymore. You know that this is true! You don't control yourself because you really don't know yourself, other than what the whiteman has taught you that you are.

The whiteman taught us that we were nothing but a bunch of no good niggas! Right? Tell the truth! He told us that we were niggas. So, just like any good slave would, we started "thinking" like niggas, and we started "acting" like niggas! Yes we did! Yes we do! Yes most of us will still think this way, even after reading this truth!

The whiteman told us that we were stupid, ignorant, and inferior to him. So we started "thinking" like we were stupid, ignorant, and inferior to him, and we started "acting" like we were stupid, ignorant and inferior!

The whiteman started treating our Blackwomen like bitches, hoes and sluts on his plantations. Soon afterwards, the ignorant and foolish Blackman started treating the Blackwoman like a bitch, ho, or a slut too, instead of the Queen mother of civilization that she is!

Yes, this is true, but wait just one minute Blackwoman! Some of you sisters were so weak-minded too, that you started to "think" and "act" like bitches, hoes, and sluts, dancing around exposing your buttocks like some devil-damned prostitute! ...and don't get mad or upset, because you know that I'm telling the truth! The only sisters that are getting upset, are the ones with there black asses hanging out for the whole world to see, right now! Don't get all upset!

Just come back correct! **RESPECT YOURSELF BLACKWOMAN!!!** And don't let any of your children around the world disrespect you, including we childish Blackmen that haven't yet grown into the fathers of civilization that we were born to be!

Now, getting back to the point, you are not in control of your thoughts and actions. Do you continue to do things that you know are wrong, but yet keep on doing them anyway!? You just sitting there wondering why you can't stop doing what you know is wrong. This is because you don't control your own thoughts and actions! You are a victim to a complex system of psychological slavery and tricknology.

The white slave-owner is still your master! The crack cocaine is still your master! The alcohol is still your master! The 40 ounce of Beer is still your master! The peer pressure is still your master! The television is still your master! The money is still your master! The girlfriend is still your master! The boyfriend is still your master! The sex is still your master! The conceitedness is still your master! The envy is still your master! The ego is still your master! The jealousy is still your master! The materialism is still your master! The credit-card is still your master! The self-hatred is still your master! The appetite is still your master! The emotion is still your master! The racism still is your master! The sexism is still your master! The foolishness is still your master! The ignorance is still your master! The true devil is still your master!!!

Everything and everybody has mastered you but your own black self. **YOU ARE STILL A SLAVE** to everything and everybody, but you ain't master to a damn thing!!! At one time, the Blackman and Blackwoman were mental-masters of the universe!!! But now, you are not even masters of your own Black asses!!!

So what are you going to do about it? When are you going to

hop the fence?   You don't even have your own names! You pride yourself in the name of the murderers, rapists, and oppressors of your people. How long are you going to be the whiteman's nigga? How long are <u>we</u> going to be the whiteman's nigga???

Think about it.

ARE YOU INTO
THAT
BLACK STUFF?

What do you mean when you ask me, "Are you into that Black Stuff?" Am I into that Black Stuff? Well, of course I am into that Black Stuff fool! As a matter of fact, I'm not into that Black Stuff, I am into this Black Stuff! Yes, I am into this Black Stuff twenty-four hours of the day. Of course I am into this Black Stuff! What else is there for this Blackman to be in, but his own Black self?

Aren't you into that Black Stuff too? I'm sure that you are. I thought all Black people were supposed to be into that Black Stuff. What else could you be into, if you are not into your own Black self? The opposite of "Black Stuff" is "white stuff". I know that you aren't into that white stuff, now are you? That wouldn't make any sense, now would it?

Why would Black people want to be into white stuff? That would be silly! So, of course I'm into that Black Stuff and you should be too! You don't have any business being into any other stuff but your own Black Stuff. This Black Stuff is your "Stuff" and this Black Stuff is my Stuff. So, get out of that other stuff and get back into your own Stuff. It only makes logical sense, doesn't it?

What if you had a cat that was into that "dog stuff"? Would

not that seem a bit peculiar? What if your cat refused to take on the thoughts, actions and characteristics of a "cat"? What if that cat just happened to had been kidnapped by some dogs when it was a kitten? What if these kidnapping dogs raised that kitten all of it's life, the same way that they would raise their own puppies? What if this kitten grew up brainwashed, thinking that it was a dog like the other puppies?

The cat knows that it doesn't look like the other dogs but, the cat tries to ignore that fact by saying that "all animals are created equal". What if this happened? You know that I am not just making all of this up, right? I mean what if this cat eventually started doing everything just like the dogs that kidnapped him? What if that cat started barking at cars and burying bones in the backyard? The cat would look pretty stupid doing that dog stuff, wouldn't he?

That cat would look pretty stupid, to other cats as well as to other dogs themselves. What if the cat went so far as to try to mate with other dogs? Have you ever seen a cat try to do that? That would look very silly wouldn't it? This silly brainwashed cat just running around trying to be a dog.

What if, one day this brainwashed cat had the nerve to walk up to another cat and say "Are you into that cat stuff?" Wouldn't that be just hilarious? This poor brainwashed cat, that thinks he is a dog, got the nerve enough to question another cat about being into that cat stuff. Wouldn't that be ridiculous?

That poor brainwashed cat needs to be taught the knowledge of his true self so that he can stop wondering why his dog companions keep doggin him around. He can try to be a dog all day long, but he will never bark just like a dog, because he is not actually a dog.

The other dogs don't really respect him. They just laugh at

the poor brainwashed cat. The other cats don't respect him, because he acts like a stupid clumsy dog. They don't want this confused animal around them either.

This poor cat is just lost, confused, and frustrated, while all the time wondering why? The cat is so deeply brainwashed that he can't see the obvious reason for all of his problems, and his downfalls. He is missing the forest for the trees, when the answer to his problem is literally right under his nose. That cat needs to take a long, long, long, long, look in the mirror and so do **you**, for asking me that dumb question!!!

TURN THE OTHER CHEEK?

Turn the other cheek? Turn the other cheek? Love your enemies? Love your enemies? We are all God's children? Say what? DON'T BELIEVE THE HYPE!!!!!

This essay is dedicated to you mentally-dead, ignorant, house-nigga, butt-kissing negroes, who are still trying to hold on to that "Turn the other cheek" ideology that has outlived it's usefulness! This is necessary, because you damn slaves won't let it die!

This a brand-new Blackman and a brand new Blackwoman! This generation will not stand for you, and your suicidal ideologies! It is time for our people to wake-up from the grave of ignorance, and you are trying to pull us back down into the coffin with you! You are dead and your ideas are dead! Well, you can remain dead-asleep, while we struggle on with the living!! We do not need your enemy-loving self! You are excess luggage! You are expendable! You have no usefulness to us, who are the righteous! Keep on loving, protecting, and defending your historical enemies! You are nothing but a two-faced, lukewarm, hypocritical slave!

Turn the other cheek? Love everybody, even your enemies? You don't really believe in that ideology, do you? Answer me honestly and directly. And don't say that you really do believe in this so-called peaceful ideology, because if you say that you do, then I would have to call you a liar and an extreme hypocrite!

You don't really believe in turning the other cheek! You are really a lying hypocrite! You will go downtown to "<u>march</u>", "<u>picket</u>", and "<u>demonstrate</u>" to the whiteman that you are a devil-damned fool, so that he can tell you "No!", to whatever it is that you are begging him for! And then he will sic his police dogs on you, and beat you in the head with his club or his "nigga-stick", while you just smiling and turning the other cheek! Every time you turn your Black cheek, he kickin your Butt cheeks!

You are just as psychotic as your enemy is! Blood pouring down the side of your head, while you just loving your enemies and turning your cheeks! You are just crazy, suicidal, idiotic, and hypocritical!

You are a hypocrite, because your "turn the other cheek" ideology, really only applies to white folks! You only turn your cheek to white folks, but you don't turn your cheek to Blackfolks! Yes, this is true and factual!

These same brain-dead negroes will come home from downtown, all bandaged-up, bruised-up, and bloodied-up, and they forget all about turning the other cheek. This same so-called peace loving, non-violent negro will become violent in their own neighborhood.

If that same hypocritical, so-called non-violent negro, was walking down the street, and I walked up to him and screamed the word "nigger!", as I started beating him with a club, this same non-violent negro would try to kill me "by any means necessary!!!"

This is the absolute truth!!! You are a hypocrite! A white man will spit in your face and you will turn the other cheek, but if a black man just looks at you the wrong way, you are ready to take his life away! You are an enemy-loving, self-hating, two-faced, confused, hypocritical, slave!!!

You mentally-lost individuals, start talking about non-violence, when it comes to your white masters! You will go and get your Bible out and start pointing to the picture of your blue-eyed Jesus! You start talking about peace and love, when you are referring to whitefolks! You start preaching about how we all got to live together in harmony and love! But, at the same time, you raising high-hell back in the ghetto! You want to live, in harmony and love, with whitefolks only!

So, you really don't believe in that so-called peaceful ideology, because you will beat up your own wife in that same day! You will beat and abuse your children until they show scars! You will violently attack your own Black brother over the smallest little conflict or reason! But if the whiteman came into your house today and kicked your big black ass, you would sit their crying like a little a cheek-turning, enemy-loving, hypocritical, Punk!!!

You are all about peace and love when it comes to your enemy, but you all about violence and hate when it comes to your own family!!! I can't even consider you to be lost anymore, because you are just a devil-damned fool, and you deserve everything that you have coming to you!

You will sit there and watch your women and children being attacked by your savage white racist enemies, and you will still sit there like a non-violent weak punk?!?! You are just a devil-damned fool, and your women and children would be damned fools to continue walking with you, after being cowardly betrayed! You need a nigga-stick upside your head! You need to be beaten by your enemies! Maybe they can beat some common sense into you!!

And don't you come to me talking about what God said and what your blonde-haired, blue-eyed, watered-down, punkified, white version of Jesus said, either!!! Don't pick up your Bible talking about this non-violent, "love your enemies", and "we all God's children" suicidal madness!!!

If you start talking like that and holding the Bible at the same time, then I know that you obviously have not <u>read</u> your Bible!!! You obviously don't know the true God! You obviously don't know the true Jesus! The true Jesus was not the punk that you are trying to make him out to be! Read your Bible! The true Jesus was most definitely not a whiteman! Read your Bible! Jesus is the Black Revolutionary Messiah!

<u>God has never loved his enemies!</u> Read your Bible! The devils are the enemies of God, and God don't love no devils! So why do you? Why do you love your enemies? Do you love devils? Well, do you? You are so devil-damned confused, by the devil in-person, that you don't know what in this hell you believe now! Read your Bible again!

Why are you non-violent towards your enemies? God is never non-violent toward his enemies! God has killed entire civilizations full of his enemies! God has killed entire nations full of his enemies! Read your Bible! God is never non-violent toward his enemies, so why are you? God doesn't turn his other cheek, so why should you? God doesn't love everybody, because God don't love devils! We are not all God's children, because the devils are not in the family of God! The devils are rebellious orphans, and nobody wants them but your silly slave self!!! So you go ahead and take care of your little wicked friends, and we will watch them take care of you!

You are just an ignorant fool! Even the beasts of the field have more common sense than you. <u>Self preservation is rule number one!</u> The animals in nature are more intelligent than you! Any animal in nature will fight to save it's own life! No matter how small the "hunted animal" is, and no matter how large the "hunting animal" is, the "hunted animal" will fight for it's life! <u>This is a rule of nature or a rule of God!</u>

You can back any animal into a corner, and it will attack you to save it's own life! **Self-preservation!!! Self-defense!!!**

You can take the peaceful being of a small squirrel, and force it back into a corner. You will find that them big buck-teeth can bite more than just acorns! This squirrel is much more intelligent than you are, with your crazy self! The laws of God and nature are right before you everyday!

That squirrel ain't gonna try to love you or turn the other cheek! That intelligent squirrel is going to try to bite the hell out of you, to get out of that corner alive! ...And if it is you, that the intelligent squirrel has come up against, he will probably bite you and then turn around and kick your ass just for the hell of it, because he heard that you were one of those non-violent, cheek-turning fools!

You are just in bad shape! You get no respect! God don't respect you! I don't respect you! The squirrel don't respect you! The whiteman don't respect you, and most of all, you don't respect yourself!

You are just a well trained house pet, or a well trained house slave. It is very rare that a dog will bark at it's master, but a dog will bark at another dog all day long.

I HAVE A DREAM!!!

"I have a Dream!" These words were made famous, when our great, great brother, Dr. Martin Luther King Jr., so eloquently expressed his vision of what AmeriKKKa should be and could be. This courageous Blackman captured the attention of an entire nation, as he stood up before thousands, in Washington D.C., delivering his most famous speech, "I Have A Dream!"

Dr. King was a very sincere and determined leader, who made great accomplishments toward the liberation of our people, but there was a problem.

There was indeed a problem. There was a problem with Dr. King's dream. The problem was that Dr. King was "dreaming" during a time of blatant "reality." Dr. King's dream was to obtain the "American Dream" for Black people, but he didn't realize that we obviously already had "The American Dream." All that Black people ever had was "The American Dream." We are asleep having "The American Dream", while white-folks are wide-awake having "The American Reality"!

We are sleepwalking Black zombies walking around in a daze, within an "American Dream". We are mentally, spiritually, economically, productively, socially, biologically, and absolutely dead asleep! "The American Dream" is your sleeping pill and your oppressors have tried to tuck you in permanently, by telling you constant bed-time lies!!!

Now, at this critical hour, we have to wake-up and look back at our mistakes from the past and learn. We have to come to the serious, objective, and honest reality, that Dr. King's methodology can no longer be used in our struggle towards liberation.

White people would love for us to hold on to Dr. King's philosophy, so that they can keep kickin our Black asses! Why do you think that white society tries to constantly shove Dr. King down our throats! They honor and celebrate Dr. King, because they want us to be "non-violent dreamers"! We have got to look at this situation for what it is and nothing else. We love Dr. King and all of his great accomplishments, but now over twenty-years later, we can no-longer uphold his early philosophies and methodology.

Black people can not continue to uphold Dr. King's philosophies any longer, because these are totally different times, that call for totally different philosophies. This is not the "I have a dream" generation! This generation is not really having the "American Dream", we are having the "Amerikkkan Nightmare"! Yes, that's right, the "Amerikkkan Nightmare"!

You know that what I am saying is the absolute truth because you were not dreaming, when you saw your youngest Black brother die instantaneously after an overdose of crack cocaine!

You were not dreaming, when you felt the cold Black barrel of a loaded pistol placed to the temple of your Black head, as you gave up all of your money, your jacket, and your shoes!

You were not dreaming, when you were running and ducking for cover from a flurry of bullets, fired into a crowd of Black people, just for the hell of it!

You were not dreaming, when your Black father walked out of the house twenty years ago, and never came back, leaving your

Black mother all alone with six Black mouths to feed!

You were not dreaming, when you heard about the little four year-old Black girl, who was killed while playing outside on the sidewalk, because she was caught between the crossfire of a Drug-War!

You were not dreaming, when you came home and found your 13 year-old Black sister collapsed on the bathroom floor, after she tried to commit suicide, because her track coach at school raped her and got her pregnant!

You were not dreaming when you frantically and recklessly drove to the hospital trying to save your Black best friend, who lay in your backseat bleeding from a gunshot wound to the neck after an argument at a party, but he was pronounced dead on arrival!

You were not dreaming, when your Black self was 10 years-old, watching your oldest brothers naked Black body convulsing in the middle of the street until he died from a heart attack while using PCP!

You were not dreaming, when your Black mother looked you straight in your Black eyes and told you that she wished that she had aborted your Black ass before you were born, because it is too much hell trying to feed and clothe you, all by her Black self!

These situations of real Black life have nothing to do with "The American Dream." This has been, and continues to be an "AmeriKKKan Nightmare" for the millions of sleeping Black people, lost in the wilderness of a strange land amongst a strange people. This is us.

Toward the end of his life, Dr. King began to wake-up into the cold and harsh realities of this world. Upon his awakening, he became a threat to the powers that be, because of his great influence over his people. The powers that be, feared that he might stop preaching "we shall overcome" and start preaching "revolution"! Their fears caused them to murder Dr. King in his prime. Now, if we begin to wake-up also, I wonder what actions would be taken against us?

Our "American Dream," of the "past", has turned into our "AmeriKKKan Nightmare", of the "present." As long as we were just asleep having a dream, we wanted to remain asleep, to avoid the reality of opened eyes. But now that our dream has turned into a nightmare, we no longer want to remain asleep. We would now do anything to wake-up and escape this constant nightmare. No sane or even insane person wants to remain asleep during a nightmare, because the only way to escape the horrors of a nightmare is to awaken and open your eyes!

So, **WAKE UP BLACKMAN AND BLACKWOMAN!** Wake up and put an end to this constant nightmare! Open your eyes, open your ears, and open your mind into the full consciousness of true reality! This is the only way to end this nightmare! We would not have been having this nightmare, if we wouldn't have been trying to dream so damn much, in the first place! Also, we wouldn't have been trying to dream, if we had not allowed ourselves to be put to sleep.

We were a nation full of sleepwalking Black zombies, but this is now the time of the awakening. It is very difficult to sleep peacefully in this strange house amongst these strange people; so awaken and arise you mighty Black Nation, arise! Arise and Awaken into the light of the sun, and escape the slumber of the devil, and his nightmare. It is all up to you. **Now is the time!!!**

BIBLE: GENESIS CHAPTER 15, VERSES 12-15

12   *And when the sun was going down, a* **deep sleep** *fell upon Abram; and lo in* **horror of great darkness** *fell upon him.*

13   *and he said unto Abram, know of a surety that thy seed shall be a stranger in a land that is not theirs, and shall serve them; and they shall afflict them* **four hundred years;**

14   *And also that nation, whom they shall serve, will I judge: and afterward* **shall they come out with great substance.**

15   *And thou shalt go to thy fathers in peace; thou shalt be buried in a good old age.*

Peace

IF THE BLACKWOMAN IS A "BITCH", THAT MAKES YOU A SON OF A "BITCH"!!!

If the Blackwoman is nothing but a "Bitch", that directly makes you a "son of a Bitch". Have you ever thought about that my brothers? The Blackwoman is not someone who you can just carelessly dis-respect, dis-honor, or dis-hearten. She is not to be "dissed" in any way. Have you lost your natural Black mind? Obviously, the answer is absolutely "YES"!

We have lost our natural Black minds, along with our natural Black eyes, Black ears, Black spirit, and Black common sense! We are at a critical time, in our history, but you fail to realize that fact, because you have lost your sense of true perception. Something is wrong with you. Something is wrong with your thinking and your vision.

So, since you are restrained by those handicaps, you don't think straight and you don't see straight. So therefore, you don't act straight, and your ignorance shows. You manifest in the form of a complete fool. Let's look at this thing.

Since when did Blackwomen become these Bitches and Hoes that you are trying to make them out to be? Where did you get that childish, weak-minded, ignorant, savage, beast-like frame of mind from? Male chauvinism is not our historical problem, so give that illness back to the fools that you caught it from!

We come from a history of "Black gods" and "Black goddesses", not "Black gods" and "Black Bitches"!!! Where in this hell did you get this crazy mind-set from? Who in this hell taught you to think on that level? You have historically had nothing but love, honor, and respect, for God's Blackwomen. So, why have you lost your minds now?

Your sisters are not Bitches, and you are not Niggas. This nigga, bitch, ho mentality is something new that you learned from your wicked oppressors. God made "Man" and "Woman"! God did not make "Nigga" and "Bitch"! So, who made the nigga, and who made the bitch? You can answer that question nigga, because you were there when the real "bitch" was made!

To understand this, we must first examine the hell of physical slavery and its psychological effects on us. The plantation is a hellified place, where hellified crimes are committed by hellified people, which has left us in this hellified condition.

But only we can get us the hell out of it, and you have to come out of this hellified nigga, bitch, ho, mentality, that was given to you by "hell" in the person of this wicked oppressor. That mentality is not yours! We have been divided and conquered. Divided from the Blackwoman, and conquered by the whiteman.

Look at the conditions of physical slavery. You would slave all day, from sun-up to sun-down. After that, you may get a chance to go to your slave-shack to eat some grits or some pork left-overs. You may even be fortunate enough to eat food with your wife or your family. This is the only peaceful time of your day.

But wait! All of a sudden the slavemasters bust into the slave-shack! Here comes Billy-Bob, Lil-Joey, and Jim-Jack breaking down the door, if there was a door! They knock the pork and grits off of the table, push you aside, and grab your wife! All three of these lust-filled, dirty, sweaty, beasts, throw your wife onto the floor and began savagely raping her right in front of your face!!!

These savage bastards are violently raping your wife and you don't do a damn thing about it because you know that you will be killed! They would do this to your wife every night, right in your face! These beasts would rape your mother or your sister of their womanhood, and rape you of your manhood, by making you watch this devilish act, while you sit there helplessly!!!

They treated your Blackwomen like pieces of meat! They treated your Blackwomen like live-in prostitutes! They treated your Blackwomen like no-good worthless hoes! And right along with all of that, they made you "Blackmen" into little, worthless, helpless bitches yourselves!

They may have "treated" the Blackwoman like a worthless Bitch, but they "made" you into a worthless, little, helpless, punkified Bitch! Yes this is the truth! I know that the truth hurts, but be a man and take it! I am talking about me too! This is us! We have to be men enough to correct our faults!

So, who is the "Bitch" now? It looks like you are the "Bitch" now! That is right, you are the Bitch, and how does it feel to be a Bitch? You sat there night after night, watching these animals savagely rape your wife, and molest your sister and daughters, while you did nothing to help them? You are the Bitch! You are the real Bitch! You have been Bitched by the white slavemaster! Yes, this is us brother.

You got Bitched so much, that you just went crazy and started trying to Bitch the Blackwoman yourself! You started treating the Blackwoman the same way that your evil slavemasters treated your wives, daughters, and sisters during slavery! You went crazy brother!

You allowed us to be divided and conquered! You allowed us to be divided, conquered, and Bitched too! You now dis-respect Blackwomen in the same way that your slavemasters taught you to dis-respect them! You were taught by their example! You were Bitched so much that you learned the art of "Bitchin"! Now, here you are still trying to Bitch Blackwomen the way that your Bitch-ass was Bitched, Bitch!

You treat your women like prostitutes and hookers!!! You treat them like sexual objects to fulfill your devilish, evil, lustful, nasty, disgraceful, wicked, savage, disgusting, perverted lower desires!!! Where in this hell did you learn that from? Who taught you that evil? What is the origin of that mentality that you now have!?!?

You learned this thought pattern from the evil slavemaster that Bitched you! You now try to call the Blackwoman a Bitch, but you were the little Bitch, when she needed your weak punkified Bitch-ass!!! How dare you open your mouth to dis-respect the Blackwoman, after all that we have been through?

Where would we be without this Blackwoman? She has been the blackbone to get us through this hellified devil-damned situation! She could not depend on your Bitch-ass! When she was impregnated by you, your Bitch-ass could not handle it, so you left her all alone! When she needed help paying the bills, your bitch-ass was not there for her! When she needed help raising "your" kids, your bitch-ass was not there for her! When she needed your protection, living in the ghetto, your bitch-ass was not there for her!!!

Where have you been Blackman? Where are you Blackman? You don't know! You probably don't know where your own bitch-ass daddy is! Do you? Where is the Blackman? Where have you been

Blackman? You probably been standing on the corner holding your crouch, in one hand, and a malt-liquor bottle in the other hand, talkin-bout how many Bitches you got! You ain't got no bitches. You the Bitch! You ain't no pimp, you just a punk!!! This is us Blackman.

Now, after reading this truth, you should not ever allow yourself to even think of dis-respecting your "Black Queens" ever again. You should never treat her like a Bitch again! It does not feel good to be treated like a Bitch. You do not want to be treated like a worthless Bitch. So, why would you want to treat your sisters like one? You know that old saying, "...what goes around, comes around." Well, what if that started happening to you?

What if the world was taken over by male homosexuals? Imagine that terrible thought. What if these homosexuals started making Bitches out of you? What if these homosexuals, put you in tight clothes, and made you dance around in their music videos? What if they dis-respectively flirted with you out in the public, everywhere that you went? What if everywhere that you went, homosexuals started coming on to you, as if you were some sort of cheap sexual fantasy?

You wouldn't like that would you? You would be ready to fight! It doesn't feel good being made into somebodies Bitch, now does it? Well stop trying to Bitch Blackwomen before somebody turns around and Bitches you! Remember that, "...what goes around, comes around."

Brothers, the Blackwoman is not your Bitch, and she is not the whiteman's Bitch! The Blackwoman is nobodies Bitch! But wait a minute! Wait one minute! Wait one minute!

Even though the Blackwoman is not a Bitch, ho, or

prostitute, there are still some of my brainwashed, ignorant, and mis-led sisters, who carry out the thoughts and the actions of true Bitches!!! Yes, that is right and I can not leave you out of the picture! We have got to tell some truth where it needs to be told.

Listen up sisters. How are you going to demand that somebody gives you respect, when you don't even respect your own damn self? You walkin around half-naked all the time. And if by chance you do decide to put on some clothes, you got to put on some slut-like, skin-tight clothes that expose every nook, cranny, and curve of your body!

You go out to these parties dancin and freakin, like a cheap ho! After the party, you have sex with anything or anyone driving a MERCEDES-BENZ or BMW! How in this hell can you demand any respect! How in this hell can you get mad at a brother, for calling you what you are obviously acting like? If you don't want to be called a Bitch, ho, or slut, then stop acting like a Bitch, ho, or slut!

Now, at the same time, this does not give any brothers an excuse to call you a Bitch, ho, or slut. Because they should just try to help you out of your sad condition, instead of taking advantage of your pitiful, disgraceful, moral-less, mentally-deceased, ignorance of self!!!

Respect yourself Blackwomen, and others will respect you no matter how ignorant they may be themselves. But do not expect respect, when you do not even respect yourself! Brothers, the next time you see a woman in tight prostitute's clothing, you should walk over to her and offer her some money, so that she will know what she looks like! Maybe she will stop dressing like a prostitute, if she starts getting paid for being one.

The Blackwoman is not to be dis-respected by anyone, not even herself! The Blackwoman is a very important link to the salvation, for all of us, so honor her. Without her, there would be no you. You are not a son of a Bitch, you are a son of a Goddess and Queen! You are much more than what you think you are, and she is much more than what you think she is!

Study-up on the Blackwoman. Once you truly understand who the Blackwoman is, you will be surprised and ashamed of yourself at the same time. Do away with your foolishness. Respect yourself and respect your origin, because if the Blackwoman is a Bitch, that makes you a son of a Bitch!!!

Peace

LIGHT, BRIGHT, AND DAMN NEAR WHITE!

"Your mama so Black that she always get marked absent at night school!" "Oh yea? Well, your mama so bald-headed that she gotta roll her hair up with rice!"

"All of yall mamas just big, Black, and bald-headed! They just plain ugly! You got a big-old, black and greasy, cornbread and neckbone looking mama! Yo mama bout as Black as the bottom of a Southern country skillet! She got all of them tight naps pullin on her head! Yo mama hair so nappy, that she got a constant headache! She need to do something about all of them naps! She probably can't afford to get her hair fixed! She need to go shop-lifting and steal her one of them Do-It-Yo-self kitchen-perms from the grocery store! Man, yo mama just in bad shape! Where did your father find her ghetto looking ass anyway?

Man, I'm not gonna mess up like your father did. I'm going to find me a good looking woman. She gonna be real light-skinned, with light colored eyes. She can't be all Black and burnt looking, like your mama! My wife is gonna be mixed! My wife is gonna have long straight hair all the way down to her butt. Since she is going to be mixed, her hair is going to be naturally straight. She ain't gonna have no problems with no naps, like your mama does.

My wife gonna have that good hair! All of my kids gonna have good hair too! Naturally curly! Also my wife ain't gonna be all hefty like your mama. She gonna be skinny like them white girls on T.V. and in them magazines. Hey, and if I go to college, I can probably pull me one of them white girls for a wife! I heard that them college white girls love the brothers, especially if you play basketball or football!!!"

Okay, so did the language of the preceding several paragraphs sound familiar to you? Did that sound like the opinions of somebody you know? Did that sound like the opinions of yourself? Have you ever made statements similar to those? I used to think like that back in the days of extreme, extreme, ignorance. I was obviously a brain-dead devil damned fool, with no knowledge of truth and self.

Our people were directly and indirectly taught to hate their natural <u>Black</u> selves. <u>Black</u> is bad! Wear white to weddings and <u>black</u> to funerals! Devil's food cake is <u>black</u> and angel's food cake is white! If I know something bad about you, I could <u>Blackmail</u> you! You can tell a little white lie, but you better not tell a big bold <u>Black</u> lie!

Our people were conditioned to hate everything about themselves that was natural and <u>Black</u>. We hate our Black beauty because we were taught to define our own beauty according to these white, anglo, caucasoidal, european, westernized, beauty standards! So this means that anything less than "blue eyes and blonde hair," is considered less than beautiful! The further you get away from "blonde hair" and "blue eyes," the uglier you get.

This is what we were taught! This means that if you got <u>Black</u>

eyes, Black hair and Black skin, you are the ugliest thing on the planet! Well if this is true, why are those crazy white folks laying out in the middle of the sun, trying to get their skin darker, when they ain't gonna get nothing but skin cancer? How in the hell do they plan to conquer the universe, and run from the sun at the same time? Silly fools!

Your Blackness is hated around the world, but most of all it is hated by you. You want blue contact lenses so that you can look more like the blue-eyed people that hung your black ass from a tree! You want light skin so that you can look more like the people who murdered hundreds of millions of your Black foreparents and dumped them into the Atlantic Ocean between Africa and AmeriKKKa!

You want straight long hair like a white woman, even though she was the one left horny and lonely, while her own savage white husband was in the slave-quarters raping one of his Black nappy-haired slaves!

Why do you want to look like these psychotic, murderous, cold-blooded, rapist "mutha-fuckas"? Yes, I said rapist "mutha-fuckas", and that was no slip of the tongue! I am just telling you the truth! Rapist "mutha-fucka"!

A "mutha-fucka" is an individual who is the "fucka of muthas"! The whiteman is a historical "fucka of muthas", around the world! A historical rapist! He was the fucka of your fore-muthas and the fucka of my fore-muthas! That is why we come in so many different shades of Black now! The blood of this rapist, "mutha-fucka" is in all of us! Don't you ever forget that! And don't you ever forget how it got there!!!

If somebody raped you tonight and they had on a "green sweater", would you go out tomorrow and purchase a whole wardrobe full of "green sweaters" to look just like the person that raped you?

Hell no! You wouldn't do such a crazy thing! So, why do you bend over backwards to look like the people who have historically murdered and raped your foremothers, and continuously rape your mutha-land of all it's mineral riches?!? You are just as crazy as they are, and where did you think the word "mutha-fucka" originated from anyway? Here you are, the <u>Original People</u> of the Universe, trying to look like the <u>original "mutha-fucka"</u>! And don't think that I am being vulgar! Because your white slavemaster has earned that title! <u>The original "mutha-fucka"</u>!

Yes I'm talking to all you sisters out there. I don't blame you for your ignorance of the past, but now that you know the truth, let the truth make you free! Let the truth make you free from that so-called "beauty-shop" appointment on Saturday.

Now that you know the truth, why would you keep on burning your scalp? Why will you keep on frying your hair? Why will you keep on bleaching your hair or dying it to a lighter color? Why would you continue to put harmful chemicals on your scalp, while knowing all the time that your scalp has pores?

Have you ever thought for a second that these chemicals can get into your pores and therefore into your system? If they do, then what vital body organ might the chemicals get into first? Is it your brain? Have you ever thought about that?

Have you ever thought about the reason that doctors tell you not to put chemicals in your hair during pregnancy? Maybe it is because the chemicals can get into your system and harm the unborn child! If these chemicals can effect the health of your child, do you think that these <u>same</u> chemicals can effect your own health? Think about it.

After hearing this truth, don't continue being the same slave-mentality-having nigga that you were yesterday! Open your beautiful Black eyes and be the beautiful Black gods and beautiful Black goddesses that you were born to be! Don't run around here trying to look like your historical enemies!

All of these beautiful Blackwomen running around looking crazy with these "temporary" permanents in their heads. Your straight hair is "temporary" but you are "permanently broke" because you are trying to get your hair fixed every two weeks, as if it was broken in the first place! Don't try to fix what ain't broken! Who told you that your hair was broken anyway? Stop looking like fools, while white folks just laughing at you because you trying to look like them! You are making a fool of yourself!

If you saw the majority of white women out here trying to make their hair nappy, you would think that they were crazy! What if white women, all of a sudden, started spending close to a thousand dollars a year, individually, on chemicals to make their hair nappy? Add up how much you spend a year to get your so-called broken hair fixed!

What if white women started spending all of their money trying to get braids, dreadlocks, twists, or just basic naps, because they wanted to look more like you? Wouldn't you look at them as if they were crazy? Don't you think that they look at you crazy? They would look like fools doing that foolish thing, and you do look like fools doing that foolish thing.

So my dear sisters, please be your black self and keep your natural black beauty, because God didn't make a mistake. God didn't make a mistake when making your strong, bold, and beautiful naps, as opposed to weak, limp, and lifeless strands of hair. Your Creator made your beauty naturally unique! Your Creator wanted your Black natural beauty to stand out amongst the peoples of the world!

God is trying to tell you something about your uniqueness! Have you ever noticed that all of the peoples of the world have limp straight hair? White, yellow, red, brown and some jet Black people have straight limp hair. But why did The God make the hair of your tribe of people unique? Nobody has your unique texture of beautiful hair, but what is The God trying to say? Why does the Bible describe Jesus as having hair like lamb's wool, in the Book of Revelations? Black skin and hair like dried raisins. Why does God want to make that uniqueness of hair more than clear to us?

The God didn't make any mistake by making our beauty super-natural! When we dance, it just comes natural to us, but it is super-natural to white folks! When we sing, it is just natural to us, but to white folks it is super natural! When we slam-dunk a basketball, it comes natural to us, but it is super natural to white folks! When we talk slang, it comes natural to us, but it is supernatural to whitefolks, how we devise new words for communication on a daily basis!

How we have survived, in this society, under centuries of oppression is a natural thing for us, but whitefolks think that it is super-natural how we have survived all of these centuries of this **Black-Hellacoust**! Yes, we die, but we also multiply! If they just break a fingernail, they fall out in the floor having a nervous breakdown! Emotional weakness.

Our thick lips are natural to us, but supernatural to whitefolks! Our strong kinky hair is natural to us, but it is super-natural to them! Not even their strongest chemicals can keep our hair permanently straight!

Our buttocks, are natural to us, but to them they are supernatural! Yes we can wear a pair of pants without a belt! Our strong noses and wide nostrils are natural to us, but they are supernatural to whitefolks! Yes we can breathe freely, and we don't have annoying nasal voices! Our historical greatness is natural to us, but to them it is <u>supernatural</u>! The sphinx and pyramids were just natural to us, but to whitefolks it is <u>supernatural</u>! Our Blackness is natural to us, but to whitefolks it is a <u>supernatural</u> phenomenon!

Black people be your <u>supernatural</u> beautiful black selves! God didn't make any mistakes, so don't you! God didn't make any mistakes, so don't you! The <u>God</u> didn't make <u>any</u> mistakes, so don't <u>you</u>!

Peace, **Black**

WELL, SPEAK OF THE DEVIL!

Bible: Revelations, Chapter 6 - Verse 8

"And I looked, and behold a pale horse: and his name that sat on him was death, and hell followed with him. And power was given unto them over the fourth part of the earth, to kill with sword, and with hunger, and with death, and with beasts of the earth."

...SPEAK OF THE DEVIL! THE DEVIL! THE DEVIL! DON'T PLAY! DON'T PLAY WITH THAT! DON'T PLAY WITH THAT TERM, "THE DEVIL"!!! THE DEVIL AIN'T NO JOKE! THE <u>REAL</u> DEVIL AIN'T NO JOKE! DON'T LAUGH AT THAT ! DON'T LAUGH AT THE DEVIL! HIS HELL AIN'T NO JOKE! THE HELL YOU CATCHIN AIN'T NO JOKE! THIS IS THE <u>REAL</u> HELL! THIS IS THE <u>REAL</u> HELL, WHETHER YOU KNOW IT OR NOT! YOU ARE A VICTIM WHETHER YOU LIKE IT OR NOT!

WELL, SPEAK OF THE <u>REAL</u> DEVIL, NOT THE <u>RED</u> DEVIL! THE ONLY <u>RED</u> DEVIL IS A <u>SUNBURNED</u> DEVIL! THE <u>REAL</u> DEVIL IS THAT WHICH YOU CAN SEE! THE REAL HELL IS MANIFESTED RIGHT BEFORE YOU, BEHIND YOU, AND ALL AROUND YOU!!! TAKE A REALLY GOOD LOOK AT THIS WORLD, THAT YOU ARE IN!!!

DON'T PRETEND TO NOT KNOW <u>WHAT</u> I AM TALKING ABOUT!!! DON'T PRETEND TO NOT KNOW

<u>WHO</u> I AM TALKING ABOUT! I KNOW THAT YOU KNOW, AND YOU KNOW THAT YOU KNOW! RIGHT? WELL FOR THOSE OF YOU, WHO WANT TO IGNORE THE FACTS OF YOUR OWN LOGICAL INTELLIGENCE, AND ACT LIKE YOU DON'T KNOW, ASK THE QUESTION!

ASK THE QUESTION, "WHO IS THE DEVIL?"! ASK THE QUESTION, "WHERE IS HELL?"! ASK THESE OBVIOUS QUESTIONS, AS IF YOU DON'T ALREADY KNOW! JUST ASK! BUT DON'T ASK ME! NO, DON'T ASK ME! YOU DON'T WANT TO ASK ME, FOR THE ANSWER TO YOUR QUESTIONS!

ASK THE PAST VICTIMS OF THIS PSYCHOPATHICAL, MENTAL-ILLNESS-PLAGUED BEAST, THAT HAS BEEN ALLOWED FREE REIGN OVER THIS PRESENT-DAY TRANSITORY EVIL WORLD.

ASK YOUR OWN ANCESTORS, "WHO IS THE DEVIL?" GO BACK TO AFRICA AND ASK THE BLACKMAN, WHO WAS HUNTED AND TRAPPED LIKE A WILD ANIMAL, "WHO IS THE DEVIL?" GO TO THAT BLACKMAN'S CAGE AND ASK HIM THAT QUESTION, THROUGH THE BARS OF THE CAGE. SEE WHAT ANSWER HE GIVES YOU.

ASK THE OTHER HUNTED BLACKMAN, WHO DIDN'T LIVE TO SEE A CAGE. YOU KNOW, HE IS THE ONE POSING IN THE PICTURE AGAINST HIS WILL, AS TWO PALE HUNTERS PROUDLY PROP-UP HIS LIFELESS, LIMP, DEAD, BLACK BODY, UP INTO THE AIR WITH TWO STICKS! THESE PALE HUNTERS WANTED TO TAKE A PICTURE OF THE BLACK MAN THAT THEY HUNTED, SHOT, AND KILLED. ASK THAT

MURDERED BLACKMAN "WHO IS THE DEVIL?"

ASK THE BLACKMAN THAT SURVIVED LONG ENOUGH TO MAKE IT TO THE SLAVESHIP. THIS BLACKMAN WAS CHAINED TO THE BOTTOM OF THE SLAVESHIP, AND CRAMMED INTO A SMALL SPOT.

TO HIS LEFT WERE BLACK SLAVES, TO HIS RIGHT WERE BLACK SLAVES, AND CHAINED ON TOP OF HIM WERE THREE MORE BLACK SLAVES STACKED. 100-DEGREES FARENHEIGHT PLUS, OF SWEAT AND HEAT. EVERYBODY'S URINE AND DEFECATION FALLING ON TOP OF HIM, WHILE MICE AND RATS CRAWL ON HIM AT THEIR OWN LIBERTY. NO SUNLIGHT, NO BATHS, FOR THREE MONTHS, TRAVELING ACROSS THE ATLANTIC OCEAN. ASK THAT BLACKMAN "WHO IS THE DEVIL?"

ASK THE BLACKMAN WHO IS ON THE TOP DECK OF THE SHIP. HE WAS THE ONE USED AS AN EXAMPLE TO THE REST OF THE SLAVES, TO ALWAYS OBEY THEIR PALE MASTERS. HE WAS BROUGHT BEFORE THE REST OF THE SLAVES, STRIPPED NAKED AND BEATEN WITH LEATHER STRAPS.

HIS BLACK BODY WAS THEN VIOLENTLY DISMEMBERED PIECE BY PIECE IN FRONT OF HIS FAMILY AND FRIENDS. EACH PART OF HIS BLACK BODY WAS CHOPPED OFF UNTIL HE LAY DEAD IN A POOL OF BLOOD, IN PIECES! ASK THAT BLACKMAN "WHO IS THE DEVIL?" SEE WHAT HE HAS TO SAY ABOUT THE ISSUE.

GO BACK TO THE PLANTATION AND ASK THE BEAUTIFUL LITTLE TWELVE YEAR-OLD BLACK GIRL,

THAT WAS JUST GANG-RAPED BY A GROUP OF LUSTING, RED-NECK, SWEATY, PALE-FACED SLAVEMASTERS IN THE FIELD! ASK HER, AS SHE LAYS THERE BLEEDING, CRYING, AND ABANDONED IN THE MIDDLE OF THE COTTON FIELD! ASK HER, "WHO THE 'MUTHA-FUCKIN' DEVIL IS?" ASK HER, WHO THE REAL DEVIL IS!!! SHE AIN'T FORGOT, YOU FORGOT!!! SHE WILL NEVER FORGET! BUT YOUR UNCLE TOM ASS-KISSING SELF FORGOT!!! YOU STILL DON'T KNOW, DO YOU? DO YOU ?

WELL, ASK THE LITTLE BLACK BOY STANDING IN THE SOUTHERN TOWN SQUARE! ASK HIM! HE JUST WATCHED HIS BLACK FATHER BEING BEATEN AND HANGED, IN FRONT OF THE ENTIRE TOWN'S PALE-POPULATION.

THE ENTIRE PALE-FACED TOWN OF CRACKAS CAME OUT TO WATCH THIS EVENT AFTER <u>CHURCH</u>! HYPOCRITICAL BASTARDS! THEY SET HIS FATHER'S HANGED BLACK BODY ON FIRE. THE LITTLE BOY JUST SITS THERE FROZEN, WATCHING, AS THE STINK FROM HIS FATHER'S BURNING BODY FILLS HIS NOSTRILS. ASK THIS LITTLE BLACK BOY WHO THE DEVIL IS? ASK HIM!!! THIS LITTLE BOY HAS YOUR ANSWER!!! ASK HIM!!! TRY TO TELL THIS LITTLE BOY YOUR LIES ABOUT A RED DEVIL UNDER THE GROUND, AND SEE IF HE BELIEVES YOUR STUPID BRAINWASHED BLACK ASS!!! GO AHEAD ASK HIM!!! TRY TO TELL HIM WHAT YOUR HOUSE-NIGGA PREECHA TOLD YOU!!!

ASK THE PRECIOUS PREGNANT BLACK WOMAN

THAT WAS TAKEN AND TIED TO A TREE NAKED! ASK HER! ASK HER, WHO WAS IT THAT VICIOUSLY BEAT HER STOMACH LIKE A BLUE-EYED BEAST, UNTIL HER UNBORN BLACK CHILD FELL OUT OF HER WOMB ONTO THE GROUND ABORTED!!! AND THIS WAS DONE FOR SPORT, FUN AND PLAY! ASK HER WHO THE REAL DEVIL IS!!! ASK HER WHO THE REAL DEVIL IS !!!

ASK THE "NATIVE AMERICAN" PEOPLE ABOUT THE REAL DEVIL. ASK THE INDIGENOUS PEOPLE OF THIS LAND, "WHO IS THE DEVIL?" FIRST YOU HAVE TO FIND ONE OF THEM TO ASK, BECAUSE THEY ARE NEARLY EXTINCT. THEIR POPULATION HAS BEEN MURDERED TO NEAR EXTINCTION!!! GO BACK IN TIME AND ASK THEM ABOUT THE REAL "THANKSGIVING"!

ASK THE WHOLE TRIBES OF NATIVE AMERICAN PEOPLE THAT WERE PURPOSELY GIVEN SMALL-POX THROUGH GERM WARFARE, "WHO IS THE DEVIL?" ASK THE YOUNG NATIVE WOMEN, WHO WERE BEATEN, RAPED, MURDERED, AND MUTILATED!! HER RAPISTS, AND MURDERS, USUALLY CUT AWAY HER BREASTS, TO USE THEM AS TOBACCO POUCHES! THIS HAPPENED TO THE WOMEN IN AFRICA AS WELL! ASK THESE WOMEN, "WHO IS THE DEVIL?" ASK THEM, "WHO IS THE DEVIL?"

ASK THE TWO-HUNDRED MILLION OR MORE DEAD BLACKMEN, BLACKWOMEN, AND BLACK CHILDREN, WHOSE BLOOD AND BONES COVER THE FLOOR, OF THE ATLANTIC OCEAN! THEY WERE THROWN OVERBOARD DURING THE MIDDLE PASSAGE, BETWEEN AFRICA AND AMERIKKKA, SO

MUCH SO, THAT THE SHARKS HAD LEARNED TO FOLLOW THE SLAVE SHIPS, TO FEED OFF OF THE MURDERED BLACK BODIES!!! ASK THEM "WHO IS THE REAL DEVIL?"

SEE WHAT ANSWER IT IS THAT THEY GIVE YOU! SEE IF THEY START TALKING THAT SAME PLANTATION FAIRY TALE TYPE OF BULL-SHIT THAT YOU WAS TAUGHT! ASK ALL TWO HUNDRED MILLION OF THEM! ASK EACH AND EVERY INNOCENT BLACKMAN, WOMAN, AND CHILD THAT LAY AT THE BOTTOM OF THE ATLANTIC OCEAN! TWO HUNDRED MILLION! THAT IS MORE THAN FIVE TIMES THE BLACK POPULATION THAT IS LEFT HERE IN THIS HELL, CALLED AMERIKKKA!

LOOK AT HOW MANY OF OUR DEAR BROTHERS, SISTERS, MOTHERS, FATHERS, DAUGHTERS, SONS, UNCLES, AUNTS, NIECES, NEPHEWS, COUSINS, GRANDMOTHERS AND GRANDFATHERS, THAT WERE MURDERED IN COLD BLOOD!!!!! ASK THEM "WHO IS THE DEVIL?" ASK THEM "WHO IS THE REAL DEVIL?"

NOW ASK YOURSELF THE QUESTION! WHO IS IT THAT KILLS WHOLE POPULATIONS OF CIVILIAN PEOPLE, AT THE DROP OF A BOMB?!!? WHO IS IT THAT COMMITS ALL OF THESE PERSONAL MASS-MURDERS, BECAUSE THEY JUST LOST THEIR JOB AT THE POST-OFFICE?!!? WHO IS IT THAT CREATED THE DEATH-PLAUGING DISEASE OF AIDS?!!? WHO IS IT THAT IS CAUGHT UP IN THIS SATANIC WORSHIPING SHIT?!!? WHO IS IT THAT LISTENS TO ALL OF THIS

SATANIC WORSHIPING MUSIC?!!? WHO ARE THE CAUGHT AND CONVICTED CANNIBALS?!!? WHO IS IT THAT SNAPS, GOES CRAZY, AND KILLS THE WHOLE FAMILY WITH AN AXE, AT THE AGE OF 14, ON A FARM IN IOWA?!!? WHO IS IT THAT PERPETUATES THIS CHILD MOLESTATION AND CHILD PORNOGRAPHY RACKET?!!? WHO IS IT THAT ALLOWS ENTIRE POPULATIONS OF PEOPLE TO STARVE TO DEATH, WHILE THEY ARE FATTENED WITH AN EXCESS OF FOOD?!!? WHO IS IT THAT MURDERS HELPLESS ANIMALS FOR SPORT, UNTIL THAT ANIMAL SPECIES IS EXTINCT?!!? WHO IS IT THAT IS DESTROYING THE EARTH'S NATURAL RESOURCES?!!? WHO IS IT THAT IS DESTROYING THE EARTH'S NATURAL ATMOSPHERE?!!? WHO IS IT THAT IS DESTROYING THE EARTH'S NATURAL PEOPLE?!!? WHO IS IT THAT IS DESTROYING THE EARTH??? WHO IS THE REAL, LIVING, AND BREATHING DEVIL TO US ALL???

WELL IF YOU DON'T KNOW BY NOW, YOU WILL NEVER KNOW! DAMN SELL-OUT!!!

Bible: Revelations, Chapter 6 - verse 8

"And I looked, and behold a pale horse: and his name that sat on him was death, and hell followed with him. And power was given unto them over the fourth part of the earth, to kill with sword, and with hunger, and with death, and with beasts of the earth."

GOD THE GANGSTA!

Hold up, hold up, wait, wait, wait a minute! Now let me ask you a question! How you figure you can out gangsta The God!?! Do you really think that you all that hard? Do you really think you all that and this, this and that? Do you really think that you have punked more punks than the almighty Black God? Please give me a break and give yourself a break! Mr. Gang-Banga, listen up brother.

You think you all hard cause you "think" you got control over a few city blocks! But, The Black God got control over every 196,940,000 square miles of this entire planet Earth! Every square mile of this Universe! You the "drug-lord" on your corner, while The Black God is "Lord of the Worlds!"

You can't out gangsta God! I'm tryin to tell you! So, you wanna ride down the street wit yo crew or yo set, tryin to be so hard! You wanna ride by intimidating people until you find somebody weak, to punk!

But all The Black God gotta do is shake the ground a little bit, during an earthquake, and punk everybody! Everybody get punked during an earthquake! You all on you knees talkin bout some, "Oh God please!", when just one minute ago you thought you was the hardest nigga in the whole world!!! Everybody get punked when The Black God is on the scene! You see what I'm sayin?

During these times, if you ain't got the "right" brothers down wit you, you better watch your back. But if The Black God ain't down wit you, then you really ain't got no back! During this day of

Judgment, of the white and the wicked, if you ain't down wit The Real Black Power, you are most definitely gonna get smoked like a straight punk! You see what I'm sayin?

Nigga, you can't out gangsta God! You can't roll on your enemies like The Black God be rollin on his enemies! You ain't killed more of your enemies than The Black God!! Here you are riding around the corner to do a drive-by shootin! You sprayin bullets everywhere and shoot-up about fifteen fools! Well, The Black God be knocking-out fools by the thousands and by the millions!!! When you read the books of scripture, you will find The Black God killin whole civilizations of devilish, wicked, punk-fools!!!

You think you "all that" cause you shot-up a car-load of niggas, while The Black God be taking air-planes out the sky with one blow! You can't out gangsta God! You bragging and boasting because you done shot-up thirty-six niggas in your time, but Black God done killed more fools than you could ever calculate or imagine!!!

God be killin whole nations of people at a time!!! God is the greatest of killas! You can't out gangsta God fool! You better make sure that you are down wit the"right" Black brother! And there ain't no Black brother more right and exact than The Black God! If Black God be for you, then can't no other punk be against you!!! Black God is the hardest brother of them all!!!

The only difference between your black-ass and The Black God, is supreme knowledge and wisdom. Black God is wise, but you ain't! Black God knows what he is doing, but you don't! Black God kills his enemies just like you "think" you do, but The Black God knows who his "true" enemies are! But you just killin up folks without knowledge and wisdom of what you doing!

Your gangsta actions are foolish, but God's gangsta actions

are all calculated, justified, and all wise! You so damn silly that you killin your own Black self! The Black God is the killa of "the wicked", but you just killin anybody! And most of you are still "wicked" your own self! Understand that <u>God is a gangsta in the name of righteousness, freedom, justice and equality!</u>

So, if you are rollin in wickedness, you ain't down wit The Black God! And that means that you are eventually gonna get seriously punked! You can't avoid gettin punked, if you are in opposition to the peace and power of The Black God! And I ain't talkin about no damn spook in the sky!

If you wanna be the ultimate gangsta, then you need to roll wit the hardest Blackman of them all!!! The Black Gangsta God of Freedom, Justice, and Equality, <u>slaying wicked punk fools in the name of righteousness!!!</u> You gotta slay the "peace-breaker", before you can be the "peace-maker"!!! You can't out gangsta God, so why try?

This is the real, living, Black God! God The Gangsta! <u>God the Killa! The Killa of the Wicked</u>!!!!!!!!!!!

Peace

WHY DO NIGGAS BE KILLIN NIGGAS?

Is the question really that difficult to answer? I don't think so. Think about it. Think about the last time that you killed somebody. Why did you kill that person? If you actually took the time and effort to kill somebody, why would you do it?

Did you kill that person because you liked that person? Did you kill that person because you were in love with them? Did you kill that person because you admired that person? No! You killed that person because you "despised" that person! You killed that person because you "disliked" that person! You killed that person because you "deeply hated" that person in your heart! So, why do you think, niggas be killin niggas?!!?

All around the world, niggas are hated as soon as they come to birth! So don't wonder why niggas hate themselves. For centuries niggas have been getting killed for no reason at all! So don't wonder why niggas be killin themselves, for no reason at all. 365 days out of a year, niggas are being disrespected! So don't wonder why niggas have no self-respect.

Generation after generation, people said that niggas ain't no damn good! So don't wonder why niggas have no self-confidence. Nobody ever loved a nappy headed nigga! So don't wonder why niggas straighten and bleach their hair.

We have all been taught that a nigga can't be nothing! So

don't wonder why niggas don't amount to nothing. This world is holding niggas down! So don't wonder why niggas pull each other down.

A nigga ain't worth a damn!!! So I don't give a damn about a nigga!!! I hate niggas just like everybody else, even though I see a nigga every time I look in a mirror! I hate all niggas! I hate good niggas and I hate bad niggas, cause I just hate niggas! I hate niggas with a passion! Every time that I even think about a nigga, I just get pissed-off!!! Because I know that a nigga is always up to no good!!! There ain't no nigga that ain't no criminal!

Every time I hear the word "criminal", I see a nigga in my mind! Every time I hear the term "crack-addict", I see a nigga in my mind! Every time I hear the term "drug-dealer", I see a nigga in my mind! Every time I hear the word "prison", I see a whole bunch of no-good nappy-headed Black niggas in my mind!

I hate what a nigga is! I hate what a nigga looks like! I hate what a nigga acts like! I just hate Black niggas! I hate Black niggas! I - hate - Black - niggas! I hate all black niggas and I can't wait to squeeze the trigga!!!

I can't wait to squeeze the trigga on a no-good Black nigga!!! I got to be a killa!!! I wanna killa nigga!!! I'm just a nigga killa!!! A Black nigga killa!!! See a nigga, kill a nigga! And all I see is Black niggas! So I'm steady on the the trigga!

So white man, you better digga big ditch, cause I'm gonna kill a nigga and I might kill his bitch!!! I hate all niggas, whether they walk like a pimp or if their wrist be limp! I'm steady pullin the trigga, on another Black nigga! And ain't no guilt on my head, cause its just another Black nigga dead!!!

A nigga be me, and I be a nigga. I hate a black nigga. And I be a nigga killa. So I'll put the gun to my own head and I'll squeeze the trigga. POW! I just killed another Black nigga.

Think about it, nigga.

IT AIN'T THE WHITEMAN FAULT!

Okay, so let us get to the root of things. You and I must be honest with one another. Black people, we should understand one thing clearly. The white man has been the number one blood-shedder, mischief-maker, and hell-raiser on the planet, but wait! He has murdered millions upon millions, upon millions of innocent people, but wait! He has destroyed the earth's natural atmosphere, but wait! But wait!!! Wait one minute Blackman! I must say one thing. The whiteman is not your problem. Did you hear what I said? The whiteman is-not-your-problem!!!

Well, who is our problem? Because we are most definitely a problem-plagued people. Who is at the root of our many problems? The whiteman is not at the root of our problem! We are!!! **We are the biggest problem to ourselves!!!** We are at the 'root' of all of our problems!

Please remember this basic rule of life, "People will do to you, whatever you allow them to do to you." Do you understand what we are saying? It is just like dealing with little mischievous children. The knuckle-headed child will try to do, whatever you allow the child to do. If you allow the child to act a damn fool, then the child will do just that!

Well, Blackman, we have allowed our pale-faced illegitimate child to act a damn fool all around the earth! Since we allowed it, he did it to the maximum. So since you are awakening back up into the fact that you are the "FATHER OF CIVILIZATION", Blackman, you need to discipline your mischievous child. It is time for "Daddy" to spank that ass!!! It is time to bring the household out of chaos and back to order. Daddy is on his way home.

But let us get back to the immediate point. Blackman, you are your greatest "ally", but you are also your greatest "enemy". Your laziness, jealousy, ego, procrastination, passivity, fear, insecurity, ignorance, and foolishness, are the stumbling blocks that constantly trip you, and prevent you from standing up like the Blackmen and Blackwomen that you are. You are holding your self back, because you are allowing someone else to do so. Do you understand what is being said?

Tell me something. If a bully, in grade school, kicked your butt everyday and took your lunch money away, who is at fault when you are starving at lunchtime? Is it the bully's fault? Is it your fault? Who is really at fault?

Well it most definitely is not the fault of the bully, because he is just being his dumb self! It is your fault for being a straight-up punk, and letting this dumb bully take your lunch money! So you deserve to starve at lunchtime! Do you see what I'm saying?

So since the devils were allowed to rule over the earth and create this pure hell, who is at fault? Blame The God, it's his fault! Yes, it is your fault Blackman. But why did God allow it? Why did you allow this, Blackman? <u>There is a reason for everything.</u> Think on that.

"RETURN TO SENDER!"

Every since we have been on the blood-soaked soil of AmeriKKKa, we have been catching all types of hell from the hell-raiser. Yes, we have caught hell from these devils, and we have "kept" the hell that we have "caught". So as a result, we have become hell-raisers ourselves, second only to "The hell-raiser". Now it is time that we give this hell back, to whom it is that we caught it from. Return to sender.

We were not these niggas, bitches, punks, and hoes that we are today, before we were kidnapped to this country. This mentality and character does not belong to us, so we must give it back!!! Return to sender!

Give the whiteman back his damn body-poisoning addictive alcohol drinks! RETURN TO SENDER!

Give the whiteman back his damn cancer-causing cigarettes! RETURN TO SENDER!

Give the whiteman back his damn death plaguing crack-pipe! RETURN TO SENDER!

Give the whiteman back his damn needle sticking heroin drug! RETURN TO SENDER!

Give the whiteman back his damn blue-eyed contact lenses! RETURN TO SENDER!

Give the whiteman back his damn hair-straightening

chemicals! RETURN TO SENDER!

Give the whiteman back his lying, thieving, deceiving, whole damn criminal mind! RETURN TO SENDER!

Give the whiteman back his damn disrespecting, chauvinistic attitude toward women! RETURN TO SENDER!

Give the whiteman back his damn greedy, cut-throat, materialistic, sick mentality! RETURN TO SENDER!

Give the whiteman back his damn egotistical, insecure, jealous, and envious weak frame of mind! RETURN TO SENDER!

Give the whiteman back his damn "death-to-go" fast food diet! RETURN TO SENDER!

Give the whiteman back his damn care-free, sport, fun, and play attitude! RETURN TO SENDER!

Give the whiteman back his damned "have sex with anything or anyone that will lay down with you" mentality! RETURN TO SENDER!

Give the whiteman back his damn ass-backward, homosexual, indiscriminate lustful mentality! RETURN TO SENDER!

Give the whiteman back his damn blue-eyed, blonde, bimbo, brain-less, butt-less, skinny, little weak white woman! You can have that back with a quickness! PLEASE, RETURN TO SENDER!!!

Give all of this madness back to the whiteman! Give all of this "hell" back to whom it is that you have caught it from! Just because you "caught it", don't mean you have to "keep it"! Give it back! Give him back his loose, low-life morals, because they are not yours! RETURN ALL OF THAT HELLIFIED MADNESS BACK TO THE SENDER! What goes around, comes around. RETURN TO SENDER!!!

But, accept only what is your own and be only what is yourself! Accept your own divine righteous morals and be your own righteous divine Black self! And anything other than that, give it back! RETURN TO SENDER!!!

DIVORCE IS THE ONLY ANSWER!!!

Look at you! You look terrible! Look at what he has done to you! Look at what you have been reduced to! Why do you continue to take all of this unnecessary abuse? Why do you want to endure all of this pain? You are still holding on, after all of these horrible years! But, why?

You know that he does not love you at all, so why do you love him so much? He does not treat you right! He beats you! He abuses you! He uses you! He curses you! He disrespects you! He rapes you! He hates you, but you love him! Why do you love him so very much? What has he ever really done for you, besides make your life a living hell? Think about it.

When you first met him, you thought that he was a little white angel. He played that "Hollywood-role", as if he was harmless, peaceful, and a righteous little saint. You were so naive that you fell for it. You believed the hype! You got suckered by a sucker! You thought that he was so nice and sweet, that you started letting him come around your home more often.

Well, soon the reality struck you right in the face. Didn't it? Didn't it? That "little white angel", that you met at first, quickly changed into a "big white devil"! Before you knew it, this man had beaten you up, knocked you unconscious, tied you up in chains , and kidnapped you!!! Yes that's right, he kidnapped you! He kidnapped you from your own home! Don't you remember this?

By the time that you had awakened, you were already halfway

across the world, in another house that he had stolen from some other people that he tricked. He murdered most of those original residents in cold blood, and then kicked the few of them that were left out of their own house, forcing them to live on little desolate reservations. I just know that you still remember all of this! I know that you have not forgotten that quickly!

Well anyway, after all of that, he took you to this stolen house and locked you down in the basement. He fed you nothing but grits and pork-scraps to keep you barely alive! He treated you bad! He then put a gun to your head and forced you to marry him! He wanted you to be his slave-wife! You accepted, because you had no other choice in this matter! So, you said "I do!" You had to!

That was the beginning of pure hell for you, because he worked you from sun-up until sun-down. He would wake you up everyday at the crack of dawn, by screaming at you down in the basement! "Get your black nappy-headed, jungle-dancing, slave-nigger self on up these stairs and out into that backyard!!!"

He had a great big giant multi-acre garden in the backyard. You would have to pick cotton and tobacco all day long, in the hot splintering sun, all by yourself!

He wouldn't help you at all! He would just sit-down, in the shade, on his lazy flat-back buttocks, screaming at you from on the back porch! Sometimes he would just run out into the garden and savagely beat you down, because he claimed that you were pickin the cotton too slow! He would beat you constantly until you became one big bloody-bruise yourself!!! Don't you remember all of this? How could you forget? Don't you remember these days?

Well what about right now, today? You are still with him! You are still married to him! Why? Why? Why? Why? Why, are you still holding on to this psychotic maniac?!?!? Is it just because he doesn't make you work in the garden anymore? He doesn't have to make you work in the garden anymore, because he has found something else for you to do, towards his own personal benefit.

He discovered that you were talented. He over-heard you singing one of those old negro-spirituals, out in the garden, one day. So, he purchased a flashy, tight-fitting mini-dress for you, and then put you on a stage for show. He now gives you a little more spending change for your lil' purse, while **h e** is making billions and billions and billions and billions of dollars, off of **your** talents!!!

Even though he is getting filthy rich off of you and your abilities, he <u>still</u> treats you like dirt. He <u>still</u> treats you like the foot-shufflin, corn-bread and biscuit-baking, fiddle-playin slave, that you <u>still</u> are!!! He <u>still</u> abuses you in every way! He disrespects you everyday to your face, and you just take it .

All that he does, is to make sure that your stage make-up covers up your cuts and bruises, before the show begins. He doesn't want the world to really know what goes on between you and him at home in private. So you just smile, shake your booty on stage, and bring your pay-check home to this psychotic fool!!! Wait a minute! He is not the fool! You are the damned FOOL!!! **<u>Divorce is the only answer!!!</u>**

Well, well, well, I guess some of you say that the situation described, could never happen to you. Think again. That is now happening to <u>you</u>. That is now happening to <u>us</u>. I'm talking about our entire Black Nation. We have been stuck here in this strange land, amongst these strange people, for the past four hundred years. This is happening to us.

We have been forced into un-holy matrimony with an abusive, disrespecting, psychotic, evil-hearted, devilish-minded population of people. **You did not choose** this marriage, you were forced into this marriage!

You were chained-down and dragged, unwillingly, to the altar! You spent your honeymoon sweating in the sun, on the beautiful spacious plantations of Southern AmeriKKKa! Your newly wedded husband was kind of "kinky", so he brought along some "chains and leather whips", for a mixture of pain and pleasure! Pain on your behalf and pleasure on his behalf!!!

This is you, Black Nation! This is me, Black Nation! This is us, Black Nation! We are suffering from the "Battered-Wife-Syndrome"! You love him, and he hates you! You love him, and he beats you! You love him, and he disrespects you! You love him, and he exploits you! You love him, and he screws you! Yes, we have got to talk about this thing!

We have got to talk about the fact that you "willingly" allow this abuse to go on. Every once in a while, you might beg him to treat you better and respect you more. But he never does. He always says that he is going to treat you better, and he gives you all of those type of empty promises. Before long, he is **kicking** your ass again, while you are still **kissing** his!!! Yes, this is you! This is us! We must face the truth! We must know the truth, so that the truth will make us free, of our present ignorance.

Our entire Black Nation has been reduced to nothing but a cheap prostitute!!! You and me! Together! On the corner! Selling out! All of us! All of us squeezed into this little-bity red, black, and green, tight-fitting mini-skirt! It's true! It is very true! We are being exploited! We are being pimped! We are being used like a cheap, two-dollar and fifty-cent hoar!!!! This is us! This is you! This is me! I'm talkin to you, H O!!!

We are the most talented and gifted people on the face of

the planet earth! Nobody can intelligently deny that fact! The whole world follows our cultural trends! Back in the days of old, the whole world would attempt to imitate our legacy of greatness. Here in the days of hell, the whole world attempts to imitate our new legacy of ignorance. Even in our slave ignorance, we are great and are greatly imitated.

Well, the whiteman knows all of this. He knows that you and your talents are in demand, even in your present undeveloped state of mental ignorance. So, knowing this, the whiteman put a price-tag on your black behind, and put you on sale. Yes he did! Yes he did!

He has got much experience in the selling of Blackmen, Blackwomen, and Black children! He knows how to market you! He knows how to promote you! He knows how to display you! He is the "money-taking pimp", and you are the "money-making ho"! He taking all the money, while you just gettin some chump-change and a slap in the face!

Yes, I'm telling the truth about what <u>we</u> have been reduced to! We can not deny it! We can't try to hide the wig and high-heel pumps now! It is too late to be embarrassed, because everybody knew that we was a "ho" except for us! The whole world looks down at us in pity.

So now that we know it, why don't we just get up out of this stranger's bed, put our clothes back on, to cover our ignorant nakedness, and start reforming ourselves to become a respectable Black Nation again. I don't want to be a "ho" anymore! Let us tell this white pimp that we are no longer "for sale" anymore, because he can now kiss our black-ass for free!!!

Look! You have the biggest economic spending dollar in AmeriKKKa today! You have economic power, but you give it to your pimp, as soon as you get the money! You don't bring any money home for yourself. You have the potential to be one of the richest nations in the entire world, if you would just simply come together and unite with your own kind.

Why can't you learn how to "pimp" your own self and talents? You don't need a middle-man. Why don't you leave your pimp? Why? Are you afraid, like the average "ho" would be??? Are you afraid that he might "pimp-smack" you???

If he does try to pimp-smack you, don't be fool enough to turn the other cheek! You better take your little shiny rhinestone studded purse, and smack the hell out of him back!!! And then you switch your, little tight mini-skirt wearing butt, off to your own part of town! Then you can get your crazy self together.

Why don't you want to separate from your pimp? Do you love him that much? Why don't you want to separate from your abusive husband? Do you love him that much? Do you love grief? Do you love to be exploited? Do you love to be abused?

Look, in all seriousness, our Black Nation needs to separate ourselves from these strange people that have been giving us this hell for the past four centuries! We can have our own **Black president**! We can have our own **Black House**! We can have our own **Black soil**! We can have our own **Black army, navy, and marines**! We could have our own **Black schools**! We could have our own **Black farmland**!

We have **Black doctors**! We have **Black lawyers**! We have **Black engineers**! We have **Black scientists**! We have **Black diplomats**! We have **Black architects**! We have **Black scholars**! We have **Black mathematicians**! We have **Black linguists**! We have a **Black labor force**! We have **Black economic power**! But the reason that we still don't really have anything at all, is because we don't have any **Black self love**!!!

All that we do have, is working for the benefit of the whitefolks who are prostituting us, while none of it is working for the benefit of our own Black Nation. The "pimp" is gettin paid while the "ho" is gettin played.

After all of these centuries of strife, their are some of you mentally-dead, house-negro sell-outs, that still want to hold hands with the love of your life, and run off into the sunset trying to find this imaginary rainbow coalition. You will bend over backwards to try and make this so-called integration work. And the more you bend over, the more you are getting screwed by the whiteman. It is a sad fact, but it is the truth.

Face the facts. You really don't have much time. **Separation is the only answer. Divorce is the only sane answer.** There is only one logically intelligent solution, provided with these circumstances. But I guess that you don't see it that way, just like that battered-wife. Well she stays with her husband only because she really doesn't believe that she can make it on her own. She is afraid. She is silly. But, what the hell was she doing before she even met her psychotic husband? She was making it, back then, all by herself. So what is the problem now?

Well, I guess that she is just crazy now. She can't think straight anymore. She has lost her mind during this traumatic experience. She is us. She has been knocked upside her head so many times, that she has lost her sense of good judgment. Well, so have you. Well, so have we.

Divorce, is the only answer!!! Read your bible. Black Moses came to separate his people from the evil clutches of

Pharaoh's hand. Black Moses has a solution. Moses did not go begging to Pharaoh with no damn civil rights **"bill"**, talking about "..can't we all just get along?" No! Black Moses said, "Let My People Go!!!"

Black Moses did not say a damn thing about no integration! Black Moses told his people to pack their bags and get the hell out of Dodge! Black Moses was determined to leave, even if they had to cross the Red Sea! No negotiations! No compromise! No peace talks! Just walked out! Gave Pharaoh "the finger" on the way out the door! The middle!

So why you tryin to hold on to this wicked oppressor? Black Moses gave you a righteous example. Don't you know that the Bible is just a book of symbolic prophecies? Don't you know that these symbolic prophecies deal with you and this present day world? We are in this world, but not of this world. We are out of place.

When are you going to make "your" **EXODUS**??? When are you going to leave this wicked Pharaoh? Pack your bags! Pack them now! We have our own "Red Sea" to cross. We have the Atlantic Ocean to cross! Back to our original lands! The center of the world! Our throne!

We have to cross our own "Red Sea", the Atlantic ocean. The "Red Sea" is symbolic of a bloody ocean! An ocean filled with the blood of the Blackman and Blackwoman! The Atlantic ocean is filled with the murdered Black bodies and blood of over two-hundred million Black Men, Black Women, and Black Babies, who lost their precious Black lives between Black Africa and AmeriKKKa, during the middle passage between **heaven** and **hell**!!!!

Let us follow Black Moses back across that "Red Sea". Let us get back to familiar ground, and familiar faces. Or, get ready to face the chastisement of eternity. This is your day of "**judgment**". What will <u>you</u> decide? Separation is the key. Divorce is the only answer.

FRIENDLY
WHITEFOLKS??

If I was a white person living in this day of Judgement, with an entire planet full of red, yellow, brown and black people that are angry as hell at me for my many crimes and atrocities committed against them for thousands of years, I'd all of a sudden be friendly too!

I'd be shouting "We are all God's children" too! I'd be trying to marry a person of color too! I'd all of a sudden try to become a perfect saint too! I'd all of a sudden want to be your friend now too! I'd all of a sudden want to be Black too! I'd all of a sudden join your church too!

Hell, if somebody had been beating you down and kickin your black buttocks everyday for four hundred years straight, and one day you finally got fed-up with it and pulled out a loaded and cocked pistol to defend yourself against that savage person, that person would get friendly all of a sudden too!!!!!

Don't you be no damned fool and get tricked by the shrewd wickedness of this evil tricknologist!!! Whitefolks smiling at you and winking their blue eyes at you, while you just blushing like a damned naive fool! You just love the attention.

Every pet dog loves the extra attention from it's master just like you do! You ain't nothing but a pet slave dog! Black Benji! Turning tricks for smiles, winks, affection, and attention from your slavemaster! What a shame.

We have to take a look at this thing, no matter who's little feelings get hurt. You don't have to be no damn tail-waggin pet slave dog for the rest of your life! It's time for you to break the chain and do your own thang!

Now I know that you are deeply in love with your whitefolks, but we are going to have to take a deeper look at Billy, Bob, Sally and Sue. We have to see this for what it is, because all of these whitefolks, no matter how sweet they are to you, are branches from the same family tree, that don't include you and me. The only way that we are included, is if we are hanging from that tree!

They are all brothers and sisters and were born from the same womb of thought. Their deep down innate nature is the same. An actor can take on many different roles, but he or she is always going to be the same person when the show is over.

Whitefolks will openly accept you as long as you are being what they want you to be. As long as you are a watered-down, weak-minded, submissive, butt-kissing, boot-licking, fiddle-playing, corn-bread-cooking, foot-shuffling, shoe-shining, tongue-biting, porch-dancing, bent-over, house-negro type of colored person, whitefolks will love you forever and ever! Some of them might even vote for you to be their city mayor. Yes, this is true, just take a look around you.

Whitefolks are also happy if you are a ignorant, uneducated, mentally-dead, dope-pushin, dope-sellin, nigga-shootin, pimp-daddy, crouch-grabbin, malt-liquor-drinkin, cracked-out, ho-havin, baby-makin, street-dwellin, car-stealin, jewelry-snatchin, criminal-minded, ghetto-gansta, type of no-good nigga, as long as you stay your crazy black-ass in your own neighborhood!!! Niggas can only be niggas in their own niggahood.

Whitefolks love little black boys and little black girls like that because little black boys and little black girls can be controlled! Niggas and negroes are the manufactured products of these whitefolks, made in the United Snakes of AmerKKKa!

"Real" Blackmen and "Real" Blackwomen scare the hell out

of these Hollywood acting, role playing, fake-faced whitefolks! You see the snakes come out of their burrows and the devils out of their hiding places then. Your friendly whitefolks can't seem to handle no "Real" Blackwoman or no "Real" Blackman, no matter how liberal they pretend to be.

When friendly whitefolks come into contact with a real, true, alive, and awakened Blackman or Blackwoman, they lose their control. They lose their cool. They get quiet. They get nervous. They get uncomfortable. They don't know how to handle you! They are use to "handling" or "controlling" Blackfolks. But, they are afraid of a nigga that is out of their grasp of control and white domination! This is true.

Whitefolks are happy just as long as they are on the top, and your black ass is on the bottom. They do not even want it to appear that you may have more intelligence than them, or more power than them, or more money than them! They don't want to be your friend then.

They want to destroy any type of platform that may elevate you beyond themselves. They want you to be weak and low charactered like them because their misery loves company. Whitefolks hate you because they ain't you, so they want to control you and hold you down!! This is the absolute truth!

I know that you understand, because some of you Blackfolks are suffering from this same sickening mentality, just in a different form. You manifest your ignorance and wickedness in the form of Sexism.

There are some men who cannot stand to see a woman who is out of their control and domination. They seek to hold back the woman because they fear that this woman's strength may grow and develop beyond the strength (or the true weakness) of the man! The man will be friendly with his wife, until she starts to become more intellectually independent, more career oriented, and especially when she begins to make more money than him. He is not so friendly anymore, because his in-grown superiority complex is now threatened. This is the truth and this insecurity is the root to a weak egotistical male chauvinist!

He is afraid that the woman may be more of a man than he is, so he holds her down! He holds her down to control her when he can't even control his own damn self! I can't stand men like this because they really aren't men at all. They are just insecure weak punks at the core of their hearts!!! They are devils in a different form of oppression, suppression, and depression.

This madness is the same madness that the whiteman has in his sick mind. He oppresses us because he fears us. And any man that oppresses a woman, must actually fear the developed potential of that woman.

Blackman you have got to give that sick mentality back to the whiteman, that gave it to you, or else you are no man at all!!!

Now back to these hollywood-acting, role-playing, fake-faced, so-called friendly whitefolks. If you are a strong Blackman or Blackwoman, they will do one of two things. They will totally denounce you and attempt to destroy you, or they will try to ride your jock, soup your head up, and attempt to win your friendship, so that they can control or use your strength and character towards their own wicked benefits. This is their reaction. This is the truth.

If you are not a nigga, negro, or colored person under their control, you will find a totally different reaction from these same so-called friendly whitefolks, that have been smiling and winking their blue eyes at you. They are probably smiling, just to keep from laughing at our dumb black asses!

If you are accepting your own Black people and being you own Black self, you have no beneficial value to your slavemasters. So, beware of "Friendly Whitefolks" and critically analyze their sincerity, to dis-cover the hidden agenda. Accept your own Black people and be your own Black self, so that you can be of a priceless value to your own Black Nation!

CHRISTIANITY "VS." THE BIBLE

Open your Black mind for a second and be objective. Open your Black mind and try to think unemotionally for a while. Try to be totally honest with yourself while you are reading this, because you ain't fooling nobody but yourself. Open your Black eyes and picture this...

It's about 11:13 AM on a Sunday morning. The Black church is filled to maximum capacity. There are about 400 Black people all around me dressed to impress. The air conditioner is on, but it's still just too hot! The Black choir is screaming at the top of their lungs, while the Black preacher wipes the sweat from his forehead with a silk handkerchief that has his initials woven into it.

Every Black body in the Black church is swaying side to side as the Black drummer plays faster and faster! The Black emotions are running sky high! Wait a minute! The Black organist just stood up and started shouting and so did someone in the balcony! Four more Black people just started dancing in the aisle with the holy ghost!!! The temperature is getting hotter and hotter!

Oh no! the Black lady next to me just started crying and mumbling under her breath! Now her Black eyes just rolled back in her head! I know that she is gettin ready to start too! I want to move away but it's so crowded with black bodies that I'm trapped! I know it's coming! I've seen it before! She weighs about 230 black pounds She's going to blow any second now! Look out! Get ready! Take cover!! Too late!!! There she blows!!!!

The Black lady jumps up from a sitting position, straight into the air shouting "Thank ya Jesus"!! She then faints in mid-air and starts to make her decension back down towards earth! Everybody lookin-up trying to determine where she will land. I am in sort of a daze because the Black lady accidentally smacked me right in the mouth with her purse, on her way up! Everything is blurry and in slow-motion! Everybody is still looking straight up in the air wondering where it is that she will finally land, as a large circular shadow starts to form all around me, getting bigger and bigger! My vision finally clears as I look upwards to see what everyone else is staring at, but it is too late once again!!!

230 pounds of 100% pure Blackwoman, propelled by the power of the holy ghost, has just landed directly on top of me!!! I'm now lying flat on my back under a heap of Black mass and perspiration!

My Black body has gone totally numb, as I gaze up at the ceiling of the Black church, noticing the very large stained-glass window. I focus my Black vision and see three white angels with some white pigeon looking feathered wings growing out of their backs. They are butt-naked and flying around the head of a whiteman, who needs a haircut and a shave. White Jesus in the Black church.

The sun is shining through the stained-glass so bright that his blue eyes seem to glare right at me, as I close my black eyes and fall totally unconscious. I thought I died and went to white heaven. It's now 11:15 A.M. Sunday morning. The choir is still singing. The choir is still shouting. The Black lady and I are still unconscious.

Yes, I know that this sounds a bit humorous, but you Black people know that this is true. I know that every church isn't this bad, but some of our churches come pathetically close to this description. I have been to some churches that looked more like a recording studio than a place for divine study and worship.

I mean they have got loudspeakers hanging everywhere! Microphones, mixing boards, mic cables, keyboards, bongos, drums, horns, guitars, and everything!!! Yes, and they sound good too!

I heard one church choir that sounded so good, I thought that they were opening up for "Earth Wind and Fire" or somebody! Everybody was up on the floor shouting with the holy ghost! Music sounded so good I was up shoutin too, until the choir and preacher started doing "The Electric Slide" all in sequence together. I knew something was wrong then. So, I just wiped the sweat off my forehead and went home. But I must admit that we was kickin-it there for a minute.

Look, I want you to reason with me. I want us to just <u>reason</u> together. Let us try to be mature, honest, and objective about this subject. Please don't let the "truth" offend you or make you upset. The only way to oppose the truth, is to defend and uphold a lie! <u>So, I want to be on the side of the truth!</u> <u>Now, where do you want to be</u>?

Okay, so let us <u>reason</u> with this thing. Let us use our logic and <u>reasoning</u> to find the real truth, or the real <u>reasons</u>.

Now, before we find the real truth or the real <u>reasons</u>, we first must ask the real questions. Why is it that most Black people call themselves "Christians"? What is the <u>reason</u>? Why do most Black churches display the image of a white Jesus? What is the <u>reason</u>? Why are all of the angels white? What is the <u>reason</u>? Why were there no Black people at the last supper? What is the <u>reason</u>?

Why is it that, when most Black people close their eyes to

pray, they see a white God in their mind? What is the reason? Why did King James feel that "he" was holy enough to revise and issue his own version of the revealed word of God? What is the reason? Why did Black slaves, whole heartedly accept the teachings of Christianity from the same white slavemaster, that gave them pure hell twenty-four hours a day? What is the reason? What is the reason? Why are we in the terrible mess that we are in today? What is the reason? We need to know the reasons.

Now, let us attempt to answer some of these questions honestly. Most of us call ourselves "Christians" because our parents call themselves "Christians". Our parents call themselves "Christians", because their parents call themselves "Christians". And, their parents call themselves "Christians", because their parents call themselves "Christians". Is this the truth? Of course it is. But why were they calling themselves "Christians"?

They were not calling themselves "Christians" because a man named Jesus visited the slave-plantation one day, and baptized them in the waters of the Mississippi river. Jesus did not come to them in a vision or a dream, and say to them "...from this day forward, I declare you all to be Christians!"

So now, if Jesus didn't come to the slave-plantation to give us this so-called Christianity, then who did come? Who was it that gave our forefathers and mothers "these teachings" of Christianity? Who was it that taught us this?

You know who taught us this. The white slavemaster gave us "these teachings" of so-called Christianity, and we accepted these teachings with no questions asked, just like we accepted everything else that he gave us.

We accepted the sun-up to sun-down hard slave-labor, with no questions asked. We accepted our own families being broken-up and sold away, <u>with no questions asked</u>. We accepted the brutal raping of our mothers and our sisters, <u>with no questions asked</u>! We accepted the beating, dismembering, hanging, and lynching of our brothers and our fathers, <u>with no questions asked</u>! Yes, and from the same man who gives us all of this pure hell, we accepted *"his teachings"* of Christianity, <u>with no questions asked</u>. Yes, this is the absolute truth!!!

So, you know that we did not receive the "true" word of the "true" God from these people. Think about it. **Why would a white man, who spends half of his time trying to kill you and your mind, turn around to spend the other half of his time trying to bring you and your mind back to life?** That would not make any sense at all, now would it? How could the same man, who has taken on the mind, heart, and will of a devil, turn around and show you the straight and narrow path to God? Think about that real good.

Now, you would be a fool to believe anything a devil says to you about God. Right? Well, we have been nothing but fools! Yes, we have been supreme fools! I am not ashamed to admit my foolishness, because I know that confession is good for the soul, so don't you be ashamed either, fool.

Now listen!!! I don't want you to think that I am saying that their is no truth in the Bible or in the teachings of Jesus. That is not what I am saying, because the true teachings of Jesus, is not what the slavemaster gave to our people. There is truth in the Bible, if you can break through all of the "<u>symbolism</u>". The teachings of Jesus are very valuable, but that is not what the preacher has been teaching! That is not what the slavemaster has given to the preacher to preach.

Yes, toward the end of that particular historical form of physical slavery, the slavemaster let us have the Bible, but wait!

During slavery, we were forbidden to learn how to read, so somebody had to tell us what the Bible said, Right? Right. We couldn't read what the book said for ourselves.

We had to depend on what the white slavemaster told us that the book said, and you know that he has been a liar since the beginning. Either we had to listen to the white slavemaster, or we had to listen to a negro preacher that was trained by his master on what to say to the rest of us niggas! This is true!

Christianity, as we know it, is only the white slavemasters teachings of what, and who, "God" and the "devil" is. We really were never taught the true teachings of Jesus. All that we have is the teachings of the white slavemaster, with Jesus' name on it.

We couldn't read to find out, what Jesus was all about ourselves. Yes, and by the time we could read, the slavemasters teachings had made us so blind, deaf, and dumb, that we wouldn't understand the Bible even if Jesus came back and read it to us personally. We still wouldn't understand, what the man was saying to us. That's how screwed-up we are brother! That's how screwed-up we are sister!

Every Sunday the preacher reads the book and he's still talking about some heaven in the sky. Every Sunday the preacher reads the book, and he's still talking about some little redman, in some red panty-hose, red-drawers and a red cape, with a red pitch fork!

Every Sunday the preacher reads the book, and he's still talking about this glorious life to come after we all die! Every Sunday the preacher reads the book and he still will sit down to a meal of "ham-hocks", collard-greens and cornbread after church is over. Every Sunday the preacher reads the book and he still will praise and uphold the image of a white Jesus Christ.

Now, I don't want to offend any preachers. I just want to tell the truth, and anybody who is in opposition of the truth, is defending and upholding a lie. The truth is that a lot of preachers are just as blind, deaf, and dumb as we are. The blind leading the blind. A lot of preachers really aren't real teachers themselves, they just need to be really taught by a real teacher, just like the rest of us.

All of that mess that we have been taught about some spook way up in the sky, and some spook way down in the ground, just don't cut it anymore. It didn't work then, and it sure as hell ain't working now. Our people thirst for truth, but we are caught in a web of lies. So, Mr. Preacherman stop spinning that web.

We can't depend on no "Ghost God" to help us defeat the devil, because the devil ain't no ghost! See, we will call on a "Ghost God" the next time we have trouble with a "Ghost devil"! But, as for right now, it ain't no "Ghost devil" that is destroying a whole race of people!

It ain't no "Ghost devil" that distributes addictive drugs from foreign countries, to inner-city drug dealers! It ain't no "Ghost devil" that teaches our Black children to hate themselves! It ain't no "Ghost devil" that stole your black buttocks from Africa against your will! It ain't no "Ghost devil" that murdered hundreds of millions of Black men, women, and children for centuries, all the way up to the present!!!...and it wasn't no "Ghost devil" that gave you those slave-making religious teachings either. You need to start preaching about a **real God** because we are obviously dealing with a **real devil**!!!

You wouldn't know Jesus if he walked up to you and showed you his identification, along with two major credit cards! You don't really know Jesus! Jesus is the **Black** Revolutionary Messiah! That is the real Jesus that the Bible talks about!

Well, who is this whiteman that you are teaching us about?

You teachin about some whiteman walkin around in a pair of cheap sandals, tryin to bless everybody! Walking around, all humble and soft like a little weak punk, talking about "love your enemies"!

God don't love his enemies. God kills his enemies, all throughout the Bible. As Black as your people are, you still teaching us about this pale-faced punk of a man! Teach us about the Black Revolutionary Jesus of the Bible, not that long-haired hippy-looking fool that the white slavemasters lied to us about!

The Bible describes Jesus as a Blackman and nothing else. "Hair like lambs wool and feet like brass that had been burned in an oven." Stop lying to Blackpeople, Mr. Preacherman! Please! You are killing us with these lies, that the slavemaster gave you. **The teachings of so-called Christianity conflict with what the Bible says. The teachings of so-called Christianity, is not the teachings of Black Jesus!** Don't take my word for the truth, read your Bible!!

Black Jesus was not the weak, soft, hippy-looking punk that the white slavemaster "painted" him to be. Now, when I say "painted", I do mean "painted". That white false image of Jesus was "painted" by Michelangelo! Check your art history!

Michelangelo never set up an appointment with Jesus to take some snap-shots for his wallet, or to pass out to his disciples! Jesus and Michelangelo didn't even live at the same time in history! Well who in the hell is this long haired hippy that Michelangelo painted?

History shows that this hippy was Mike's relative, posing for that picture! Yes, this is the truth! I know that you believe it, because you remember how they did it in the 1950's, when they use to put pictures of white folk on the covers of record albums, but when you took it home and played it, it was the "Isley Brothers" singing on it. Do you remember that? Okay, well look at how Black people originated Blues and Rock n' Roll, but yet white Elvis Presley is the so called "King of Rock n' Roll". Do you follow the pattern?

Well it is the same thing in the Bible. A Blackman did all of the work, but they want to put a picture of a whiteman on the cover. Yes it is a shame! You got all of these pictures of a false Jesus. The false pictures of Mary and the child, were also paintings of Michelangelo's relatives. Mary was a Black Egyptian woman, and the lips and nose of the white lady on that false picture don't look nothing like the Black lips and Black noses of the statues in Black Egypt.

The Bible describes Jesus as a Blackman, and he wasn't no punk talking about "...let's work with the system and pray that we'll get justice". Hell no!! Jesus was public enemy no. 1! Jesus would hang-out with the thieves! Jesus was mocked, scorn and thrown in jail! Yes Jesus is an ex-convict! They didn't like Jesus, so they crucified him. They didn't like trouble-making niggas back then and they don't like trouble-making niggas now!

So, they nailed this Black Revolutionary man to the cross! Now, the devil got you wearing a cross around you neck with a "dead man" on it. The devil wants you to remember that if you start acting-up too, he is gonna do you like he did Black Jesus!

Why do you think the K.K.K. is so eager to burn a cross on you front lawn! They do that to remind you niggas of what happened to Jesus, the Black Revolutionary! You might end up crucified like Black Jesus! ...like Black Nat Turner! ...Like Black Marcus Garvey! ...Like Black Martin Luther King! ...Like Black Malcolm X!

These "trouble making niggas" got crucified, because they didn't want to work with the system! They even crucified Martin King, who at first was going to work with the system, but as soon as he considered otherwise, they had a cross ready for him too! Take that crucifix off from around your neck. It is a graven image. It's image reminds you of how many niggas that have been murdered and put into the grave.

Everybody is looking for Jesus to come "back", but they are not looking for him to come "Black". You wouldn't recognize him in an "X-cap" and some two-hundred dollar basket-ball shoes. Jesus is still A Black Revolutionary.

The scriptures of the Bible are not the teachings of this so-called Christianity! These teachings of Christianity were given to us by the white slavemaster. The Bible is the history/prophecy of Black folks. Read your Bible from a Black Theological perspective, not from a white Theological perspective.

After you have finished with your Bible, get a Holy Quran. In times like these, we need to have **all** of the revealed word of God, not just part of the truth. We need all of God, not just part of God. So look out, cause Jesus is coming **Black**!!!

Peace

UNDERSTANDING THE TERM "DEVIL"

When Blackfolks first hear about whitefolks being labeled as "devils", they have one of two different reactions. One person reacts in total agreement. They say, *"I knew those wicked-ass, hell-raising, mischief-makin bastards, were devils all the time!!!"*

The other person will react in total defiance. They say, *"Well that just can't be true, I know plenty of good whitefolks. I swear I do. You wicked niggas are just 'reverse-racists'!!! That is crazy talk!! I gonna tell ' Massa Jones' on all of you crazy niggas!!! And he gonna string all of y'all niggas up on that tree over yonder!!!"* These are the two basic reactions.

The person who agrees, usually agrees because they have a knowledge of world history or their own personal history, which reflects the evil of this whiteman. The whiteman has not only been raising hell with us here in this country, but with all of the peoples of the earth.

The person who disagrees, usually disagrees because of their lack of exposure to our true history. They have fallen into this fairytale frame of mind, so they dispute without knowledge, just as it is written that they would do. They dispute without knowledge. They dispute without understanding. They usually dispute from the point of view of an "over protective slave", but there are also many of us who just simply do not understand.

Well just what does all of this "devil" stuff mean anyway? What is a real devil? We do not believe in the "red-devil" with a pitchfork anymore, because when we were children we thought and understood as children, but now we must do away with these childish things. Right?

So for those who disagree with the resolution of the whiteman being the real living "devil", let me ask you a question. Since you can tell me what the real devil "ain't", can you tell me what the real devil "is"? Can you tell me what the real devil is, without giving me some type of "spooky" explanation? Remember that we are an intelligent thinking people now, and we have done away with the childish, spooky, fairytale explanations, because the type of hell that we been catching ain't "spooky", nor is it a "fairytale". It's real. And the devil that has been raising this hell is living within real flesh and blood.

So yes, I know that flesh and blood is "not" our enemy, but wait. Evil spiritual wickedness "is" our enemy, but wait. What is this flesh and blood? Flesh and blood does not automatically qualify a person to be a "devil". That would be un-intelligent thinking, just like the legacy of stupidity that whitepeople have created for themselves, by condemning Black people simply because they are beautifully **Black**.

Flesh and blood is just simply a vessel, a vehicle, or a "container". The flesh and blood is the "container". You do not judge a man by his flesh and blood, you judge him by the contents of his "container". So, let us not even look at the fact that this "container" just happens to be "pale" and life-less looking. Let us just look at the "contents" of this pale "container". What is "contained" within the brains of this pale man (or container)?

So, what is "contained" in the brains of this man?? What is "contained" in the brains of this man that he has become the absolute number one <u>killer</u> around the entire world? He has spilled the blood of every people on the face of the entire planet earth!

What is "contained" in the brains of this man, that he has become the number one <u>mischief-maker</u> around the world? His evil way of western so-called civilization, has corrupted all four corners of the globe, tempting all of the original righteous peoples towards wickedness; fractionalizing the original peoples, causing them to fight amongst themselves.

What is "contained" in the brains of this man, that he has become the number one <u>rapist</u> around this world? His weak, wicked, and sickly-seed, has been violently discharged into the sacred womb of every aboriginal woman around this earth, so much so, that his lust-filled blood slithers and courses through the veins of every people around the globe!

What is "contained" in the brains of this man, that he has become the number one <u>colonizer</u> of all the nations around this world? He has swindled, tricked, and violently threatened his way into political domination and control of the governments of the world, while "pimping" them all for their natural mineral resources and riches for his own greedy personal gain, through world-class prostitution!

What is "contained" in the brains of this man, that he has become the number one mass-murdering, bomb-dropping, women and children killing, blood-thirsty <u>savage</u> around this world? He ignorantly verifies, documents, and even boasts of his savage uncivilized behavior, within the pages of his own history books and world history classes!

What is "contained" in the brains of this man, that he has

become the number one animal-extincting, environment-killing, earth-destroying, suicidal, genocidal-maniac around this world??? So what in the hell is contained inside the internal structure of this man's brains, to provoke him to behave in such a beast-like manner all throughout his 6000 year history on this earth? What are the contents of this "pale"container?

No, the "pale flesh" and blood is not our enemy at all, because spiritual wickedness is our true enemy, but wait just one minute! Our enemy of spiritual wickedness is obviously and historically contained within the container of this pale flesh and blood! Now why is this? Spiritual wickedness is, and has been, the contents of this whiteman's historical character! Yes, you have got to realistically look at this thing. I'm talking to whitepeople and blackpeople alike!

(I know that you whitefolks are reading this too, because you have historically been nosy as hell! You all are some of the nosiest people that I have ever met in my life! But that is just part of your paranoidal nature. You could not be content in Europe, without sticking your narrow nose into everybody else's business around the world! Yes, this is you. You just nosy! What in the hell are you doing reading this book anyway? The title of this book is called "FROM NIGGAS TO GODS". You ain't the target audience! That title ain't directed toward you! You ain't the one that has been oppressed, suppressed, depressed, regressed, and digressed to the low level of mental existence, that you so eloquently termed "Nigger"! So why are you reading this book? Ain't you got anything better to do?)

Now, back to my beloved, beautiful, Black Brothers and back to my beloved, beautiful, Black Sisters, let us continue our research for knowledge of "self", "God", and the damned "devil". Please excuse me for getting side-tracked. Thank you.

History is best qualified to reward our research, so if you want to be rewarded with the knowledge of who the true devil is, just simply research world history. The whiteman will tell you all day long, that he is the devil (or 'the container of spiritual wickedness', for you soft-slave-negroes). You can read it right there in his own history books! We have just been to blind to see it! Read his own history books! He makes a record of many of his evil deeds, right there in his own "his-story" books.

He even boasts about his bloody history. He just describes his evil deeds as heroic acts of bravery. Instead of saying he stole somebody's land, like a common thief, he says that he made "great conquests" and "acquired" the land!

Instead of saying that he took-over and colonized somebody else's nation, he says that he came to "civilize" the "native people", and bring them into so-called "Christianity"!

Instead of telling you that he violently mass-murdered millions of innocent people during a war, by dropping an atomic bomb on their civilian cities, he will make himself into a hero by saying that his "skill" and "modern technology" allowed him to display valiant courage while "saving the free world" from the evil opposing forces! That is a sick mind. That is a sick man.

Yes, these little wicked devils are crazy, but ain't nobody more crazy than us for being fools enough to follow them into their foolishness, and believe the hype! This is us. The whole world was given a devil as a companion, and we all let the devil lead us straight to hell! Here we are, in this living hell with the living devil. Misery loves company. And the devil has fooled us into accompanying him in his evil way of so-called civilization.

Okay, so the typical negro slave mentality response is to say that, *"Well all white people ain't like that and most of you black people are devils too!"* Yes I've heard your weak argument before, but we must not dispute without knowledge. If you disagree without knowledge, just ask questions, or quietly contemplate to yourself until you receive the answers to your questions. But don't jump-up trying to argue on that which you have no understanding of, because you make yourself look very foolish. You jumping-up to protect your "massa", just like the porch-dancin slave that you still are. Just sit-down, listen, and objectively think.

So, yes there are black people who commit much evil in our own community. Yes, there are some evil, wicked, scheming, corrupted, devious, devilish, back-stabbing, sell-out, two-faced, non-trustable, wicked no-good niggas out here!!! Yes this is true, but wait!!! Do you truly understand why this is true about your Black people???

Your people are victims of the "natural devil". Your people were taken out of their "natural" surroundings and placed in a "strange" land amongst "strange" people for 400 years. All of the evil that we do was "learned", and is a direct result of our experiences and exposure to the "natural devil".

You are a "devil" too, because you are not in your "natural" mind state. Have you lost your "natural" Black mind? Yes you have! Yes you lost it! You had your "natural" Black mind before you got here! You have not always been the evil niggas that you are today! Historically, you were dignified, civilized, and moralized, before the white slavemaster mentally grafted our Black babies into the niggas that you see today!

This is not our nature. This evil mentality is not our natural minds. If you trace back through the life of a Black criminal, you can find the psychological effect that this oppressive and depressive life, under the rule of the devil, has had on the Black criminals's mind to drive them to lash-out in criminal aggression. That is just the hard fact. Research it for your own self. Black people are not criminals by nature, they are victims of the "natural criminal".

Now let us look at the world-wide criminal activity committed by these whitefolks. Why do they commit their crimes? Have <u>they</u> suffered from centuries of mental, physical, social, spiritual, and economical oppression??? Were they the victims of a malicious and violent "mental rape"??? Hell no!!! So, what is the reason that they commit such evil crimes around the world?

No, they were not raped of their "natural minds"! They totally have their "natural minds". They totally have their "natural surroundings", and they totally have been their "natural selves"! They are victims of nobody but their own evil selves! Nobody drove them crazy enough to do what they did to the peoples of the world! They just did it naturally, for no reason at all! This is the truth. Face the facts. Wake-up Blackman and Blackwoman! Open your eyes to the reality of this world.

So yes! You are right! The pale flesh is not the devil! It is the mind that dwells within that pale flesh. **<u>You should only judge a man on the content of his character, and judging by the content of this man's character, he has obviously got some serious mental problems.</u>**

The pale flesh is just a sign. The pale flesh is just the symbol of death. This is just the mark of the devil. All peoples of the world are some shade of color, but this one, odd, specific, particular people are set aside to themselves. Why is this? This signifies something doesn't it? Isn't there a reason for everything?

Well why did the Creator make a particular people, at a particular given time, that are "unalike" to the rest of the peoples of the world? Why? What does this mean? Why is it that these particular people have a particular mind state that is peculiar only to themselves? Why did the Creator give them a particular "unalike" exterior characteristic along with a particular "unalike" interior characteristic? Does The God do stuff just to be doing stuff? I don't think so.

In the book of Revelations, in the Bible, it talks about a "pale-horse". And everywhere this "pale-horse" traveled, hell followed closely behind, because death was riding the "pale-horse". "Spiritual wickedness" is "spiritual death". When a person dies, they become pale. Pale is the symbol and "color" of death. That is just the truth. The "pale-man" is not the devil, because he is "pale". He is "pale", because he is the devil.

So the typical slave-negro response would now be, *"That is just crazy talk! We are all God's children! We all bleed red blood! We are all the same!"* Well that is true to a certain extent, but a white shark bleeds red blood too, and I wouldn't advise you to turn your back on one of them brutal blood-suckers either.

So, now the question is, *"Well are they all devils?"* Okay, that is a good question. I once heard a wiseman say that some snakes are poisonous, and some snakes are harmless, but they are all snakes just the same. They are all made from the same nature.

Well what does this mean? What does this mean, that they all have the same nature? Well we could thoroughly break-down the biological structure of the physical bodies, or the psychological effect of the absence of key chemical hormones that are missing from the brain and blood system, of those physical bodies. We could talk about under-developed neurological systems that dramatically decreases motor-skill, sensory perception, and cognitive comprehension, potentiality and abilities. We could talk about all of that type of stuff, but this is not the appropriate forum.

So, let us just say that they all have the same nature because their minds were all born out of the same body of thinking, philosophy, and ideologies. There minds were created from the same pattern of thinking. This wicked pattern of thinking has been carried on from generation to generation for centuries and centuries. Just like the fact that, even though we are off of that early plantation, we still suffer from that slave mentality that was grafted into us back at that time. But we are gradually getting away from that grafted mentality, as we begin to accept more and more truth back into our hearts.

Well, a long, long, long, time ago, this wicked mentality was grafted into a group of original people who's physical appearance dramatically changed, because of their wicked grafted mentality. They lived thousands of years in the caves and hillsides of Europe. The teachings of death were placed into their interior heads and hearts. So now their exterior outer-covering also reflects the death that is within their hearts and minds. Death became them. As a man thinketh, so is he. As a man thinketh, so is he.

So, just as "the truth" is gradually grafting us back into our original mentality of Gods and Goddesses, there is a ity-bity, tincy-wincy, little-bit of hope for those of them who accept "the truth" also. They must be grafted back, to be successful though. But most of them will never accept the truth, because they are hypocritical liars by nature. To change their nature would be a tremendous effort. One would have to undo 6000 years of wicked mind conditioning. The reason that we are coming out of our mental condition is because we accept truth by nature. We were created in truth. So to accept truth is natural for us. But whitefolks don't want to hear truth, and most of them just don't get the point anyway.

Now as for you devil-loving, slave-mentality-having, house-niggas, this ain't no signal or cue for you to run off searching for some "good-whitefolk" to un-graft!!!! You sit your little rusty black butt down somewhere! You butt-kissing, boot-licking niggas had better turn all of your "un-grafting" energies toward yourself, you damn slaves!!!! You had better save your own slave self before you run off trying to save your devil-damned slavemaster!!!!

Fool, you better take all of your energies to cleanse your own self of the filth placed in you by this devil! And after you finish cleansing yourself of evil, you go and assist your own brothers and sisters in their efforts to cleanse themselves! Self first! Self first!

How the hell you gonna save your historical enemy before you save your own family!?!?!?!? Don't you be no damn fool, fool!!!! Save your own foolish self, first!!! You do not owe nobody no damn favors except your own self, your family, and your God!!! So stop being a devil-damned, devil-loving, self-hating slave!!! Accept your own and be your own Black self!!!!!!!!! THINK ABOUT IT.

THE VALUE OF DEVIL

Is there any value to the devil? On first thought, one may say "...absolutely not!", but, upon deeper meditation of that question, we may receive deeper understanding.   How could there be any value in the devil, to the righteous ones?

To objectively examine this, we must first rise above the strong pull of emotions, which are rooted in us, from being the number one victims of this devil. We would have to de-personalize our subjective point of view and look at it from a larger historical objective point of view. We must look at this from the eye of God.

First we must admit to ourselves, the truth of the origination of the wicked devil. Everything in creation has originated from God and the devil is a part of that creation. God made devil. This is the painful truth. The devil is not self-created. God made that wicked devil. So, why would God do this to us? Why did God allow this hell and hardship to fall upon us?

God allowed this to happen, so that we could become a wiser and stronger people. We were to be made stronger through the test of endurance, here in the jungles of Far West Asia (AmeriKKKa). We have had to endure, mentally as well as physically, the hellified condition of living under the rulership and dominion of this devil in his hell. This is the true hell and it is truly hot for those who struggle against the wicked in-justice of this true devil. Have you ever heard the phrase, "I feel like I've just been through hell and back!"? Well this will be a common phrase among our people once we completely make an Exodus out of the beastial bowels of our oppressors, because this is hell.

The God has allowed the devil to totally de-construct the Blackman and Blackwoman down to their lowest level of being, so that we can now be reconstructed and resurrected under the direction and will of our Black God. We are being re-formed, re-shaped, and re-made, under the supreme creativity of the Creator.

Whenever something is to be re-formed, re-shaped or re-made, it must be melted down first, by extreme heat and fire, such as with metals, plastics, and glass. After this hellfire or heat, The raw material can be made into a different form shape or make. It can be made new. It can be made better, depending upon the will of the maker. Do you understand?

The Maker is The God, and he has allowed the heat and hellfire of this devil to melt us down to our lowest quality of existence, so that he can re-form, re-shape, and re-make us into the highest quality of existence and become the supreme wonder of this world.

God made man from Black mud. Jesus made a bird from dust. The Creator will make us into gods and goddesses from niggas. Remember that the great pyramid, in the land of our ancestors, was once a pile of un-organized, un-formed, un-shaped, un-made, material, but now it is one of the scientific, architectural, mathematical, astronomical wonders to this whiteman's world!!!

The devil was created by God to put us through hellified trials and tribulations. These trials and tribulations were to make us a much stronger people than most. We had to be "nailed to the cross" of material affliction and spiritual death, before we could receive the "crown" of material justice and spiritual life.

The God put us through this hellfire at the hands of the devil. Do you truly understand the value of the devil? This evil world is a transitory world from one point of history to another. The devil's rule was given only "6-days" or six thousand years to exist over the world. Six thousand years is a drop in the primeval ocean of infinite ancient Black history. This is like a preparation period to take us from one point of development, to a higher point. This is like God's form of "boot-camp".

God hired the devil to put trial and tribulation on us during this hellified "boot-camp", so that we will come out as mighty soldiers for The God. Soldiers of truth! Soldiers of righteousness! Soldiers to kill anything and everything that is unjust and wicked. And looking at our people today, this "boot-camp" has most definitely hardened and toughened us up as warriors. But we are now only making war with ourselves. This has to stop, of course.

Let us use a brief example to support this entire point. Imagine two kids at the age of five years-old. One lives in the ghetto and the other in the rich part of town. The ghetto child grows-up under horrible conditions. No family. No father. No money. Violence, crime, and poverty is everywhere that he can see. He grows up on the hard city streets and learns to survive amidst all of the death and destruction around him. This is just his way of everyday life.

Now on the other hand, the rich kid grows-up with every luxury in the world. He has a maid, a nanny, a butler, a family, money, and everything else. He has always been pampered all of his life and got everything he wanted. He had no problems at all. He has never suffered from any struggle, trial, or tribulation.

So now he has grown-up to inherit his family riches. But now all of a sudden at the age of 25, he goes totally broke! He carelessly and foolishly loses all of his money and hits rock bottom. And at the same time, the brother from the ghetto, who is also now 25 years-old, just won the state lottery! He struck it rich overnight!

The brother from the ghetto, moves to the rich neighborhood, and the rich guy, who is now poor, has to move to the ghetto. Yes that's right, a flip-flop situation.

Well now, which one of these twenty-five year old men do you think will survive in their new environment? That answer is obvious. The young man who grew up under struggle, trial, and tribulations in the ghetto, is strong enough to survive anywhere! But the young man who grew up in the rich neighborhood, who never suffered anything, will not last at all on the ghetto streets.

He is too weak to endure any hard life conditions, because he is not prepared for that. He has not been through the ghetto boot-camp before. He has been developing 25 years of "weakness", while the brother from the ghetto has been developing 25 years of "strength". Do you understand?

We as a Black Nation have been developing four whole centuries of strength, just building and building. It amazes the devils that we have survived such trial and tribulation. We are still hanging tough even after all of the external and internal pressure that has been devilishly put on our people. No other people could have survived and continue to survive the greatest human tragedy in the history of the planet, **The Black Hellacoust!!!**

There is actually no type of value at all to the devils. But there is much value to the way that God uses the devils to make us stronger and wiser. We have to learn how to be patient with the wise God. His actions and plans may sometimes look totally wrong to us. But if we divorce our emotions and rise into the mind of God's thinking, we may better understand the master plans. God is the master planner and best knower.

Peace

WICKED-ASS
BLACK DEVILS!!!

I want to talk to you. I want to talk to those of you, who take "delight" in calling the whiteman a "blue-eyed devil". It's time for you to take it to a deeper level.

You would make a terrible, fatal, and grave mistake to think that the whiteman is the only devil. That would be childish, unintelligent, and foolish to assume that. Don't be superficial in your thinking.

Think about it. Think about all of these statements deeply. What is a devil? <u>A devil is a wickedly rebellious person. A devil is a wickedly rebellious person that is in constant opposition to truth and righteousness. The opposer of truth. The rebel of righteousness. A devil.</u>

This means that <u>anybody</u> with a wickedly rebellious mentality towards truth and righteousness, can be labeled a "devil". This means that a devil can manifest in the form of a whiteman, Blackman, male, or female. Remember, that "flesh and blood" is not your enemy. It is the wickedly rebellious mentality that lives within that "flesh and blood", that is your enemy.

When you hear people saying "the whiteman is the devil", you need to understand what that means. It is not the "<u>pale</u>" flesh that is the devil. The flesh does not harm anyone. It is the diabolical, wickedly, rebellious mind contained within the "pale" flesh. <u>The "whiteman" is the symbol, and the "white-mind" is the substance</u>.

This wickedly rebellious mentality against truth and righteousness, has been alive and dominate among the masses of white people throughout their history. Their history is a story of chaos, murder, and mischief written in pure blood.

But, as you know, white people and their peculiar mentality have traveled to every corner of this earth. And they have taught their rebellious mentality, or thought pattern, to the rest of the world. They have spread their mental disease all over this world.

They have reproduced themselves, by reproducing their mentality in other people. They seek converts to their wicked mentality and way of life. So now the earth is filled with wicked devils, and the earth has become a hell or home to these devils. Hell is our abode. The earth has become a habitation of devils.

We, Black people in AmeriKKKa, have allowed ourselves to be raised by this devil's hand. Therefore the devil has been our teacher and we now have the devil's mentality. If you think like a devil, you become a devil. "As a man thinketh in his heart, so is he". We have been made into **Wicked-Ass Black Devils**, even though that is not our true nature, under <u>natural</u> circumstances. This is true.

The whiteman was genetically grafted out of the weaker recessive genes of the Black Original Man. So, this means that everything of evil, that you recognize within the whiteman, comes directly from the potentiality of your Black self. You have the potential for this manifest wickedness within yourself too, and so do I. So the whiteman works night and day, through his media, to pull this wicked potential out of us Original People, because their wicked misery loves our company. His world of media is used to tempt, provoke, stimulate, and lure us down into his wicked mental condition. We fall for this tricknology all the time, and become our own worst enemy, the devil.

Wicked-Ass Black Devils. They seek to destroy the righteous, just like any other devil. Study the whiteman. Study his mentality. Study his rebellious thought pattern. Master what you have studied, and learn it well. Once you have learned the characteristics and thought pattern of this mentality, you can recognize any kind of devil.

You can recognize a white-devil, black-devil, red-devil, or blue-devil. Once you lock-in on the mind of the devil, you can recognize the devil coming in any shape, form or fashion. Once you locate the mind of the devil, you beat it down with truth until it dies. Truth kills lies. The mind of a devil is based on a lie.

The whiteman ain't got to do nothing to you personally, he will just send some of his mentally-grafted Black devils out to do his wickedness. So don't think that you can recognize a devil, just based on his skin color. Skin color is a "sign", the mentality is the "substance".

A self-hating, suicidal, sell-out, wicked-ass, Black Devil, slave nigga, will kill, lie, cheat, steal, and back-stab you to death, if you are not careful. He or she was taught personally, by the "great deceiver" in the person of this whiteman. This is of the times.

Learn that mentality. Learn the devil. Know the devil. Know that mentality. Be wise in your thinking. Go past the symbol, straight to the substance. Be on guard against **Wicked-Ass Black Devils** too. But most of all, be especially on guard against that wicked black devil inside of you. PEACE TO THE RIGHTEOUS.

GETTIN

F'D-UP!

Everybody wanna get (effed-up) f'd-up! Every single weekend we got to get f'd-up out of our minds, as if we ain't f'd-up out of our minds already! We are displaced out of our normal mind-state! Everybody gotta get "f'd-up"! Everybody wanna get "ripped"! Everybody gotta get "blunted"! Everybody tryin to get "high" in one way or another!

"Yo, just bust open the 40 oz. of brew and let the joint smoke, or let the blunt toast!" Whatever we do, I just wanna get "high"! But Why? Why do I wanna get "high" all the time? Why? I like to get "high" because it makes me <u>feel</u> good!

But why does it make me <u>feel</u> good? It makes me <u>feel</u> good because it puts me in a different mind state. All of my problems just disappear wit a couple of puffs, and a few bottles of beer. I feel like a brand new person. I got courage, strength, and a worry-free mind! That's why I like to get "high"! Because I get a brand new "high" state of mind. I can escape from the realities of myself and my life! But, if it feels so good, why do we call it gettin f'd-up?

We call it "gettin f'd-up", because you feel f'd-up after you come down from that temporary chemically induced "high" state of mind. The "come-down" part is the f'd-up part! To wake up the next morning with a hangover, is the f'd-up part!

So, now you gotta get f'd-up again, just to forget how f'd-up you feel from gettin f'd-up last night, because you now realize that you f'd-up, when you decided to get f'd-up in the first place! That's really f'd-up! That's why we call it "gettin f'd-up"!

So once you make that first f'd-up decision to get f'd-up, you start a f'd-up cycle of dependency or addiction. So, as a result, your whole life can become f'd-up, and the lives of your family and friends can become f'd-up too, because of your f'd-up situation. Your finances will be f'd-up! Your relationships will be f'd-up! Your health will be f'd-up! Your future will be f'd-up! So, when you decide to start gettin f'd-up every weekend or everyday, you should understand how f'd-up you are actually going to get, before you make that first f'd-up decision.

But now, let us understand why we want to get "high" all of the time anyway. We want to get "high" so that we can escape our reality. We want to have a good time, but we can not have a good time if we see reality for what it is. So I have to distort my vision of reality to forget my real misery.

The whiteman is a smart psychologist in the science of tricknology, so he knows this. This is why he will put you in a hellified condition of life, and then hand you a crack-pipe so that you can artificially escape your reality of hell. This is the easiest way to make a nation of addicts.

You want to get "high" artificially, because you feel "low" in reality. People who are already secure within themselves and feel good about themselves naturally, do not need to get f'd-up. They are secure within, and they love themselves too much to do any harm to themselves. But if you are not secure within yourself, and you suffer from subliminal self-hatred, you don't care about "gettin f'd-up", because you really believe that you don't deserve anything better.

True? True. That's f'd-up!

It is even more interesting to look at this subject even closer. What is the real reason we Black people want to get f'd-up or get "high"? Well when we consume these various forms of drugs, we are actually trying to artificially achieve a "spiritual frame of mind". We consume these products to feel "high" or achieve a "high" state of mind.

Gettin f'd-up is actually a spiritual thing. Yes that's right, I don't care how hardcore you think you are. That is the truth! You are actually trying to achieve a "spiritual frame of mind", when you are drinking alcohol or puffin on a blunt or whatever. But don't confuse being "spiritual" with being "religious", because they are two totally different things.

Spirituality is a "high" state of mind and a "high" state of being. That is why if feels so good when you are on these drugs. You are trying to get back to the "high" spiritual frame of mind that we sustained and maintained when we were gods and goddesses, before our fall.

But now just wait one minute, because there is a major problem. Don't think that this justifies you for gettin f'd-up all the time. Don't get crazy. I don't wanna hear you talking about, "...yo man, I gotta toast-up this blunt so I can mentally hang-out with the ancient ancestral gods and goddesses out by the pyramids, so that we can exchange intellectual concepts on the mathematical dimensions of inner space." Nope, I ain't tryin to hear all that.

We must understand that when we "artificially" attempt to induce this "high" spiritual frame of mind, it does harm to our natural physical and mental systems. Our body takes devastating injuries due to these artificial stimulants. These products are made to trigger a chemical reaction in our brains, but it is artificial, because it is stimulated by an outside influence. This is why we suffer so badly when we come down from the artificial high. It is not natural. So, it doesn't have a natural effect on the body.

But on the other hand, these different levels of "high" spiritual states of mind and states of being, can be achieved naturally. We can trigger these same chemical reactions to an even higher degree, naturally. This is the high frame of consciousness that we maintained on a constant basis when we were divine Black gods and goddesses, before our fall. This natural state of "high" had a positive effect upon our being, instead of the negative effect brought on by these artificial stimulants.

Our ancestors achieved this constant "high" frame of mind, through "Black melaninated excellence." We achieved this through supreme knowledge and supreme wisdom. We maintained a constant level of "peace and power" by being obedient to the laws of nature or the Universe.

Now don't let this spook you out because of what white-folks have taught you. I'm serious. We were getting in tune with the universal cosmic flow of energy. You can't get a higher buzz than that! And you ain't got to come down off of that! And you ain't got to pay for that! This is also called submitting your will to the Creator's will, or getting in touch with your "higher" self. This is achieved by "study" and living a life of righteous virtue. This is achieved by maintaining a constant quest for perfected self-construction.

Now, I know that some of you are too hard-core for all of that and you can't break your gangsta image, but listen to what is being said anyway. You ain't gotta be soft to be spiritual! You ain't gotta be no punk to be down wit the Creator! Nigga you ain't harder than The **Black** God!

I know that you see all of them punks and sissys in religion, but them punks and sissys don't know the true God! They think that God is a pale-faced, long-haired, blue-eyed, sandle-wearing, flower-picking punk! That's what the white slavemaster taught them brainwashed fools! The God that I'm talking about is **Blacker** and Harder than all of you wanna-be-gangsta-niggas put together!!! You can't out gangsta God! Nigga please!!!

If you want to be on a constant high and hang out wit the hardest gangsta on the block, you need to hook-up wit the hardest "**Black** Peace" and the hardest "**Black** Power" that the whiteman has been trying to keep you away from, for centuries. Since you are already trying to achieve a spiritual frame of mind artificially, you might as well go straight to the **Black** source of real spirituality. Getting "high" ain't always gotta be f'd-up! Come on and let's go from NIGGAS TO GODS!!!

PEACE, **BLACK**

THE FRUIT DON'T FALL TOO FAR FROM THE TREE!

Okay, so how should we approach this thing? I want to express a few viewpoints from this perspective. Take an objective look, and an objective listen.

Well, I am fortunate enough to receive the opportunity to talk with many older people. I thoroughly enjoy talking with older generations because they have a lot of knowledge and wisdom to pass on.

But too often, I run into older people who sustain a prejudice. They sustain a prejudice against the younger generations. I'm not talking about "all" in the older generation, but "some". Sometimes this prejudice even seems to be kind of bitter. And when I sense this prejudice, I become disappointed, because I see that we are being divided and conquered, one generation from another. What a shame.

I hear a lot of older people say to me, "you seem to be an

intelligent young man, but the rest of this generation is just worthless." How can they say this? This is working on my nerves. I guess they expect me to jump right in, and start talking bad about the people in my generation too! But I can't do that because my generation is me, and I am my generation! And I love me, so I love my generation. These older people just don't understand. The older people, that try to disrespect us because of the condition that we are in, just don't truly understand. I don't like to hear people condemn us without the proper understanding of our present day condition.

All too many times, I hear older people describe our generation as nothing but a group of drug-dealers, crack-addicts and gang-bangers. Damn, are they believing the hype or what? Yes, I know that our generation has many, many, many, many many, serious problems but wait! wait! wait! This does not mean that the older generation should attempt to dis-own us! This does not mean that the older generation can just wipe their hands clean, of us! This does not mean that the older generation can act like we did not come directly from them! The older generation should never forget, that <u>the fruit don't fall too far from the tree!</u>

That's right! You have to re-think this whole thing because you are our mothers and our fathers! We did not come out of the womb acting a damned fool!!! We were your babies, but somewhere along the way, <u>you</u> allowed somebody to teach us how to be a damned fool! Now don't think that I am placing all of the blame on you, because we will, and we do take responsibility for our own selves. And of course we know where all of the ills in our community stem from.

But, at the same time, you cannot attempt to separate yourselves from us. We came from you. You gave birth to us. So before you cast a stone at us, take a look at yourself. If you examine your own weaknesses, you just might understand where we received our weaknesses from.

I was not <u>born</u> a pimp! I was not <u>born</u> a permiscuous prostitute-like slut! I was not <u>born</u> a hopeless, crack-pipe smoking addict! I was not <u>born</u> a trigga pullin nigga killa! I was not <u>born</u> a drug-dealin money lovin fiend! I was not <u>born</u> a street-dwellin, malt-liquor drinking, crouch holding, trouble causing nigga! I was not <u>born</u> this way! You cannot put all of this on just me! I did not come from the womb doing these things! I had to <u>learn</u> it from somewhere! I had to <u>learn</u> it from somebody! Children only <u>imitate</u> their atmosphere! We only <u>imitate</u> our surroundings! Yes, so we were born in sin! And this world of sin was here before we were born into it! We are just merely <u>products</u> of our atmosphere! <u>Products</u> of the times! <u>Products</u> of you.

Please do not condemn us without proper understanding. This is what "<u>our</u>" enemies want you to do. They want you to disrespect us, so that we can disrespect you back. We have been divided and conquered enough. We are all one big broken family, but a wound can always be healed with the proper <u>care</u>. But if you all don't <u>care</u> about us, then the wound will become deeper and deeper and that wound will continue to spill precious Black blood, needlessly.

Whitefolks done got you scared of your own kids! They have put all of these images on television to scare you away from your own children, and for a particular reason too, but we will discuss that later.

Yes, I know that we have EVIL in our eyes and that we will curse you out for little of nothing, but wait. You have to understand. <u>We are angry as</u> hell! We are mad as hell! We are upset! Think about it!

Look at this world in this present condition! We were born

right into the middle of this extreme chaotic madness! Wouldn't you be highly upset if you were born right in the middle of this mess? We come to birth, and can't even have a decent life or a decent chance to live. Just a child, and can't even see a future, five years, two years, one year ahead! Don't wonder why we have an attitude on our faces twenty-four hours a day! I'm upset! We are upset! You should be upset too!

Don't let "our" enemies divide us up! We are yours and you are ours! All that we ever wanted was a little love anyway! All we ever wanted was a little attention! All that we ever wanted was a little respect! All that we ever wanted was love!

But white folks and their media hype got you too scared to even look at us! And, on top of that, white folks got you to start condemning us too! You are helping your enemies to push us into the grave! You are helping to kill off your own children! You are killing yourself, because we are your future! Stop trying to <u>abort</u> us! You <u>made</u> us! So <u>deal</u> with us! <u>Keep</u> us! <u>Respect</u> us! But most of all <u>love</u> us!

Most of you don't see our value at all. But white folks see our value, and that is why we have been targeted Public Enemy NO.1!!!! Even though we have all of these problems on our backs, we are still kickin hard! White folks can tell that this generation is the strongest of the strong!

After all of the crap that our people have gone through, we have produced a generation that has a cold hardened heart, and they do not take much abuse, before they go-off! Whitefolks see this and get scared! Because <u>these</u> negroes are not able to be tamed! <u>These</u> negroes will not bend to become the whiteman's slave and servant!

We say if we got to be a negro, servant, or slave, then we

don't want to be nothing! So, as a result we have become wild, tameless, and aimless. And whitefolks do not like having blackfolks around, that are out of their immediate control. This alarms them. So, if we can't be tamed, then they seek to kill us, by any means necessary.

A Blackman is of no value to them unless he is a slave to them, or unless that Blackman is playin a fiddle and shufflin barefoot on a whiteman's front porch for entertainment. If you are not one of those two, you are worthy of death to him. Understand that.

This is the type of generation that Blackpeople have been waiting for. This type of generation is what we need. This is a fearless generation! This is a cold-hearted generation! And the whiteman had always ruled us through fear and the weakness of our natural warm, soft heartedness. All that 'love your enemies' type of psychotic madness will get you killed. And this generation don't love nobody because don't nobody love this generation, and unfortunately we don't even love ourselves.

So how are we gonna love thy enemy? You must be a damn fool to think that we gonna be turning the other cheek? So, we ain't going to be doing nothing but fighting with those who fight with us! Uncle Tom is dead! and if we find him alive, he's gonna wish he was dead!

This is the generation that you all have been praying for. All that we need is a little guidance, love, and respect. We were born with a quickened, excited, independent type of rebellious spirit, that is of a great value. We look like a bunch of fools, but we are the key to the salvation of this Black Nation. You have not been wise enough to see that we are of a very great value.

You must remember that everything that we do, we learned it from someone else that was already here. Yes, this is absolutely true.

This behavior is <u>learned</u> behavior.

We <u>learned</u> how to do a "drive-by shooting" from AmeriKKKa, when she did a "Fly-by" shooting on Libya, Panama, and Iraq! We gun down our black people just like AmeriKKKa has gunned down the yellow, red, brown, and Black peoples of this earth all throughout history. This ain't nothing new!

We make our money through illegal "buy and sell" activities, just like the illegal activities that this country's richest families, and business people, have used to succeed, for themselves. This is nothing new. **We only <u>imitate</u> our atmosphere.** So, for those who don't like what they see in us, take a good look at <u>yourself.</u> THE FRUIT DON'T FALL TOO FAR FROM THE TREE!!!

This generation of people are of great value and are the strongest of the strong. So give us the love, attention, and respect that is due, so that we can return the same back to you. <u>We are yours and you are ours.</u> And <u>we</u> <u>are</u> <u>all</u> <u>we</u> <u>got.</u> So let us become <u>one</u> generation, with <u>one</u> common goal. "Total liberation for the whole entire Black Nation." The older generations have **survived,** so that this generation can now **succeed**. We respect you. We honor you. We love you, and we thank you.

"RATHER DIE LIKE A MAN, THAN LIVE LIKE A PUNK!!!"

Nobody! Nobody!! Nobody!!! Nobody, knows nor do they understand what goes on in the mind of a Blackman!!! The enormous pressure, stress, and pain!!! It is outside of description!!! It is beyond articulation!!! It defeats all intelligent comprehension!!!

Me and my brothers. My brothers and I. We suffer the pain of death, even though we are considered physically still alive. We are the walking dead! Alive without a purpose! Death becomes us! Death became us. Dry bones of what once was.

The depth of our minds go undiscovered. The depth of our thoughts go unshared. The intensity of our pain goes un-vented. But now we have reached the threshold, and our cup runneth over in **ANGER!!!**

All of the pain, frustration, humiliation, and bottled-up, un-expressed, centuries of pure anger have been passed-on to the present generation of young Blackmen! Pulsing through our veins! Swelling in our hearts! On the brink of massive explosion!!!

How many more generations of Blackmen did they think would take this shit, with no questions asked!?!? Somebody is obviously going to have to give-in to justice or DIE! Talk to the Blackman today and explore his thoughts! Ask him how many times, has he orgasmically dreamed of killing those who kill him!!! Ask him! He knows the truth that is deep in the seat of his pounding heart!

How does it feel to be a man, that is not <u>allowed</u> to be a man? This is dreadfully painful! This is the pain of death! This is being buried alive with your eyes open, spectating your own funeral! Having so much power, but not being able to exercise your innate divine power! Being a witness to so much evil, wickedness, and destruction, but yet not being able to do a damn thing about it!!! This is a pure hell for the Blackman!

How can I describe it! How can I explain what this feels like? It feels like a once mighty fiery bird, that now has it's wings clipped and its fire extinguished! It's like being a big Black strong "Mike Tyson", with your hands tied-up, while some little wimpy, watered-down, weak, white, pale, pissy-punk, is kickin your black ass constantly, and there ain't nothing you can do about it!!! This little devil just pimp-smackin the hell out of you!

Put you in some tight little lace pants and then making you dance around on his front porch! You wigglin and dancin like a little "freaky-deaky", while this little devil is laughin his ass off and your wife is cryin her eyes out!!! How in this hell do you think this makes the Blackman feel?

It's like having a nuclear bomb in hand while some little punk-bastard is whooping your ass with a sling-shot!!! I am a man, but can't be a man? I am a man, but I can't be a man!?!? This is the way of this world! This transitory evil world! These six-days! These six-thousand years! "The whiteman's heaven is a Blackman's Hell."

I can not fully describe this pain, although I have tried. If a man can not even support and protect his own Black family, he feels totally worthless. Since he can't be a man the "right" way, he will try to be a man the "wrong" way.

He will be a pimp, to "<u>feel</u>" like a man. He will be a gang-banga, to "<u>feel</u>" like a man. He will beat his wife and kids, to "<u>feel</u>" like a man. He will be a domineering male chauvinist, to "<u>feel</u>" like a man. He will copy-cat the whiteboy, to "<u>feel</u>" like a man. He will kill other niggas for no reason at all, except to "<u>feel</u>" like a man. He will attempt to sex every woman in the world, to "<u>feel</u>" like a man. He will sell-out his own Black people, to receive acceptance in the whiteman's world, to "<u>feel</u>" like a man. He will kill, steal, wheel, and deal for material possessions, to "<u>feel</u>" like a man. He will seek the praise of his peers, to "<u>feel</u>" like a man. He will do anything to just, "<u>feel</u>" like a man, even though all of this madness ain't got nothing to do with true manhood! But to "<u>feel</u>" like a man, and to "<u>be</u>" a man, are two totally different things.

The Blackman just wants to be a Blackman. <u>The Blackman just wants to be a Blackman</u>. That is all that he truly wants. This Man just wants to be a Man. He just wants to be himself again. His manhood was violently castrated away, in order to allow these devils to rule for 6 days (six-thousand years). The Blackman would not allow this, otherwise. This was in the plan.

This helpless pain can not last forever and ever. The elders and older Blackmen say "...son that's just the way it is. That's just the way of this world." Well my response is "...sir, <u>with all due respect</u>, I am in this world, but I am not of this world. And I, personally, am sick of this **slave shit**!!! So that's 'just the way it is' for you, but I'll be damned, or I'll be dead if that's just the way it is for me!!!" "I don't care if everybody in the world say I got to live like a damn slave! If that's the case, then every single last one of you can kiss my **Black ass**!!!"

I myself, personally, wasn't made in the image and likeness of no devil-damned slave!!! I just ain't made that way! I can't be bending, bowing, begging, butt-kissing and boot-licking for no damn crumbs from the whiteman's table!!! I was made in the image and likeness of The Black God! I ain't yo Nigga!!! And I ain't no Nigga!!! This is truth! This is me! This is us. This is my generation!!!

I fear for the man who pushes the button! I fear for the man who pushes the button of this generation! I fear for the man who pushes the button of this generation, that will unleash the swelling, boiling, building-wrath of the Ages!!!

It only takes one push on the one right button and this Black volcano shall erupt into a mountain of fiery "Blackness" that shall devour everything wicked that strays into it's path!!! I fear for the man who pushes that button! This is a new time! This is a new day! This is a new Blackman and Blackwoman!

So the wise whiteman better go talk to the ignorant, dumb, hill-billy, red-neck whiteman. You better talk to your brother. You better keep him away from that button.

You are wise and you know the real deal, so you psychologically train us Blackfolks to turn this "wrath" inward on ourselves! But now your bag of tricks is running-out. We are slowly, but surely waking up. And we are not _ever_ going to forget the nightmare. So, now what? Now what? How wise are you? Are you really wise?

Will you voluntarily remove your buttocks from the seat of power or will you wait to be removed? How long did you think this was going to last? How long did you think that you could run around the house wearing daddy's clothes? You better take a look out the window, because daddy's coming home. So will you be wise, by taking daddy's clothes off before he gets upstairs, or will daddy have to do it himself? I wonder? Are you really wise? Times-up.

People should understand this new generation. They don't want to live with the whiteman. They don't want to work for the whiteman. They don't want anything to do with the whiteman. They want to be with themselves, be amongst themselves, be for themselves, and be themselves. They want to be Blackmen and Blackwomen.

They were not made in the image and likeness of slaves. They just are not made like that. They will even sell drugs to be independent of a slave job. Entrepreneurship is the key, but we need to sell products that are healthy for our people, not self-destructive. This is just mis-directed and mis-guided energy.

But how can we know, except we have a teacher? And how can we have a teacher except, he be sent? Don't send me no damn teacher from the whiteman! Don't come to us, if you just a negro representative of the whiteman! Send me a Black teacher, yes! But, send me a Blackman, from a Blackman! Send me a Blackman from The Black God!!! Only a "true" Blackman can reproduce a "true" Blackman.

This is the only guidance that can control the power, energy, or spirit of this generation! Everybody else just better step-back and step-off! This is the rebirth of the Original Blackman and Original Blackwoman! The second Adams (Atoms)!

This is not the "Turn the Other Cheek" generation! That is over and gone! That is not our slogan! Our slogan is **"I'd Rather Die Like A Man, Than Live Like A Punk!!!"** This is our slogan! This is our ideology! So don't push the button, lest you write a check that your ass can't cash!!!

"I'd Rather Die Like A Man, Than Live Like A Punk!!!" This is our slogan! This is our ideology, because we are dying anyway! We are dying everyday, in the streets of AmeriKKKa anyway! We are dying over silly-stupid type of shit anyway! So don't think that we will not die for the liberation, and salvation of our Black Nation!!! Please give yourself a break! We ain't got nothing to lose!

We already losing our lives! So what the hell? I'd rather die for a "cause" than to die for some "crack"! I'd rather die for a "cause" than die for some "crack"!!! Think about it! I'd rather die for the red, black, and green, than for a red or blue gangsta color! And I, most definitely would rather die for the red, black, and the green, before I would die for the red, white and blue! I'd rather die for a "cause" than to die for some "crack", and I'd rather die for a "cause" than to die for some "crackers"!!!

So for those that are wise, you already know this. You should not press the button. Don't press the button, if you are as wise as you "think" you are. If you are truly wise, you know who made us like this. You know who fathered our minds this way. You know who is backing us. "The" Original Man. Time's-up! "I'd Rather Die Like A Man, Than Live Like A Punk!!!" What have we to lose? Nothing! Not a damn thing, but this misery of slavery. Rather die like a man, than live like a punk.

Black Power to The **Black** People!!!
A KIL!!!

!RELIGIOUS CONFUSION!

"My religion is this!" "My religion is that!" "My religion say this!" "My religion say that!" "Well I'm a Christian!" "Well I'm a Muslim!" "Well I'm an original Black Jew!" "Well I'm an Egyptologist!" "Etc., Etc., Etc.!"

My dear brothers and sisters please stop all of this madness! Just hush your mouth! Just shut-up! Stop! Wait! I don't want to hear all of this mess! Can't you see what this unnecessary confusion is doing to us? Are we going to be divided and conquered <u>again</u> by this white man's petty labels and titles that he put on us? Answer that question!

Okay so let us look at this thing. So you say that you are a "<u>Christian</u>"? Well <u>so am I</u>, because I'm trying to grow or 'crystallize' into the mind of the "Christ" too!

So you say that you are a "<u>Muslim</u>"? Well <u>so am I</u>, because I am in submission to the will of God too!

So you say that you are an "<u>Original Black Jew</u>"? Well <u>so am I</u>, because I am an original Blackman who is circumcised of the heart too!

So you say that you are an "<u>Egyptologist</u>"? Well <u>so am I</u>, because I am the Black seed of that great civilization, and every Black god and goddess that ever lived, is wrapped up in my very DNA genetic coding, alive and well, living within the sub-conscious mind of my spiritual third eye, waiting to exhibit and express supreme powers of divine too!!!

You can't separate yourself from me! I'm not going to let you do it! I am your brother! And I'm not going to let these petty labels, titles, and names separate me from my strong and beautiful Brothers or my strong and beautiful Sisters! You are mine and I am yours! I love you and you love me! I don't care what we "call" ourselves, because we are all Black and catching hell because of it!!!

We were all created in the nature of righteousness, even though circumstances have made us disobedient to our true original nature!!! Yes, we are made of many different Black "atoms" (Adams), but we come together to form ONE "solid Black Body" of people!!! God is ONE! And his people are ONE!!!

Please do not fall victim to the traps of this whiteman-made "Religious Confusion." The devil is the author of this chaos and confusion. But God is the author of order and clarity. If you find your mind being twisted in a knot, then you know that the devil is involved. Think about it.

Where is the best place for a devil to hide? Where is the last place that you would look for a devil? Well the best place for a devil to hide is in religion, and the last place you would expect to find a devil is in a church, mosque, temple or synagogue!

If you are not careful, you could end up with a devil trying to teach your congregation the path to God! Oh well, we have not been too careful, and so now we have had a devil as a companion and teacher. No wonder we are so confused and in chaos. The devil has led us astray from the ONE path of God, onto all of these many different paths that lead straight to the confusion and chaos of this devil's HELL!!!

"Well my religion say this and my religion say that." Oh just be quiet slave! Don't tell me what "your religion say". Tell me what <u>you</u> say!!! What do <u>you</u> have to say about the matter!!! "Well my preacher say this and my teacher say that." Well if you have been learning something as a student of your preacher or teacher, <u>you</u> should now have something to say for <u>yourself</u>. So tell me what <u>you</u> have to say!

"Well my religion is this and my religion is that." Oh just be quiet! You can't separate yourself from me! Don't pay so much attention to the <u>labels</u> and <u>names</u> of your religion. That is not important. Don't take pride in labels. <u>Take pride in your level of wisdom, knowledge and "living" spirituality</u>.

And don't ask me what my religion is, because you just can't wait to label, title, or stereotype me. I'll just answer you by saying that my religion is the religion of <u>truth, freedom, justice</u> and <u>equality</u>!

Now what you got to say? Now are you going to be in opposition to that? Is yo religion be different from that? If I gave you a label for my spiritual teachings, you might pre-judge me and dispute against me without knowledge! So the name of my religion be "TRUTH"! Now what be the name of yo religion, since you want to be so different and separate? Anything that places itself in opposition to "TRUTH", can be nothing more than a "LIE"!!! So the name of my religion is "TRUTH"! Now are you with me or without me? Think about it.

We have allowed these damned devils to divide and conquer us in all of this religious chaos and confusion! How did this mess get started? Each prophet of divine did not come here trying to confuse us! Each prophet or messenger did not come here to teach us different religions from different Gods! These teachers of divine all came teaching <u>one</u> message and <u>one</u> message only!

They all taught <u>one</u> religion! They all taught us to be <u>obedient to the will of THE ONE GOD!</u> They all taught us to be obedient to the ONE WILL of TRUTH! They all taught us to be obedient to the ONE WILL of RIGHTEOUSNESS! They all taught us to be obedient to the ONE WILL of JUSTICE!

And for those who "claim" that they don't believe in a God, the prophets and messengers were teaching us to be obedient to the Laws of Nature! They all taught us to be obedient to the Universal Cosmic Flow of Energy! However you want to phrase it, all of these teachers, prophets, and messengers of divine, all taught "One" message!!!

So don't tell me about your prophet and I won't tell you about my prophet, because your prophet is my prophet and my prophet is your prophet, as long as they are teaching "TRUTH"! The only difference between one prophet from another is the level of wisdom that they bring to us.

Each messenger or prophet just brings to us a deeper understanding of the same TRUTH. God decides to deepen our wisdom as we can mentally handle it, and as we grow in our understanding. "The master appears when the student is ready." We just graduate from one teacher to the next, but they are all in the same school of thought. The school of TRUTH. Ye shall know the TRUTH, and the TRUTH shall make you free!

We could always express our "religious rituals" in different ways, but never forget the commonality of our "spirituality". We are all rooted in the same spirit of truth. Do not magnify our differences. Magnify our similarities! We are all rooted in the same spirit of truth! The same spirit of truth animates all of the righteous ones, just like pure electricity.

Electricity (spirit) is constant. It just changes forms of expression, depending upon the vessel in which it manifests its power. Electricity animates a television, and electricity animates a microwave, but the electricity just manifests its power differently through each vessel. But they are both electrical appliances. They are <u>both</u> electrical appliances. They are <u>both</u> of the same source. They <u>both</u> live from the same energy. Do you get the point of what I'm saying?

<u>We are all of the same source</u>. The same energy. The same spirit of truth and righteousness. The only <u>true separation</u> is going to be of "<u>the righteous</u>," from "<u>the wicked</u>"! Not "the righteous" from "the righteous!" Let us cast away the <u>chaos, division</u>, and <u>confusion</u> created by this <u>devil's tricknology</u>! Black people open your eyes, ears and mind to realize the reality of your commonality!

We all share the same origination and therefore the same destination. We - all -share - the - same - "origination" and - therefore - the - same - "destination." Think about it.

Peace

"ENVY, JEALOUSY, AND EGO"

I once heard that a very wise, all wise, most wise, truly wise, supremely wise, master of a person said, "Accept your own, and be yourself." At the time that I first heard that statement, I did not fully understand the infinite depth behind those words. But as the day grows long, I am beginning to understand more and more. So, stay tuned.

Now, let us talk about Envy, Jealousy, and Ego. ENVY, JEALOUSY, AND EGO! **ENVY! JEALOUSY! EGO!** Yes! Let us talk about this thing once and for all! These three diseases plague our people very deeply. Envy, Jealousy, and Ego. These three cancerous infections have always plagued our people! This is why we constantly stay divided.

These terrible infections are but symptoms of an even deeper disease, that we suffer from, which is pure **"insecurity" or "low self-esteem"**. This is our **root problem.**

Envy is motivated by not being confident with what you got, so you got to be envious of what somebody else got. Jealousy is developed, when you are not truly satisfied with who you are, so you become jealous of who somebody else is. Ego manifests itself, when you feel insecure about your own true character, so you front a perpetrated false character, like you are somebody important, because deep-deep-deep-down inside, you really believe that you are nobody and nothing important. You are considered to be a subliminal hypocrite. Think on that.

To solve our problem, and to cure this spiritual disease, we must do **one** thing! We must, **"Accept our own and be ourselves!"** That sounds like two things but it is actually only one thing. To accept your own, is to be yourself, and to be yourself is to accept your own.

Black people, we have allowed envy, jealousy, and ego to keep us divided for a very, very, very, very, long time. This is an extreme weakness among our people. The wicked of this world, have used our weakness, to divide and conquer us, since the beginning of their time.

This is the same weakness, by which they keep us divided and conquered. They understand that we will always continuously give birth to a "Jesus" type of character/person, to combat their wickedness. But they also know that we have always also produced a "Judas" type of character/person, to sell-out our people and work on behalf of the wicked devils. All that the devils have to do, is put the "Judas" on their payroll for a few pieces of silver.

But, we must understand that the "Judas" doesn't necessarily sell his people out just for mere material wealth. That is the surface of the matter. But what is at the root of his evil motivation??? ENVY, JEALOUSY, AND EGO! EMOTIONS! INSECURITY! This is the root of the evil motivation. We must not only look at what the "Judas" is doing, but we must also look at why the "Judas" is doing what he is doing.

Black people are sick to the core with this bitter, deadly, suicidal spiritual disease. Yes, this is true! Just listen to our language!

How many times have you heard these statements that I am about to say?

"Who dat nigga think he is? He ain't nobody!" "Look at her stuck-up ass! She need to sit her lil' black stuck-up ass down somewhere!" "He always tryin to act like he better than somebody. He ain't nuthin but a no-good nigga, just like the rest of us niggas! That nigga ain't bout shit!"

Black people this is our everyday language, towards one another! I know you, because I am you! The whiteman ain't gotta hold us down! All the whiteman gotta do, is say that he likes one of us better than the other one, and we fools start fighting and arguing with each other, while the whiteman is sitting there tickled pink! Literally! He just sits their mentally manipulating us fools, while he just laughing the rest of his diminishing flat buttocks off.

Black people, we hold each other back! The whiteman controls us through psychological warfare, by using our emotions to make us self-destructive! This way, he can get rid of us poor, silly, dumb niggas, without getting his hands bloody anymore.

It is quite clear that Black people are just like a bucket of crabs. We all trying to pull each other back down. Everybody wants to be somebody, because we all have been nobody for so long.

We know, deep-down inside of us, that we are supposed to be a great people, but circumstance has not provided us the proper atmosphere in which we can manifest this innate greatness. So, now everybody wants to be "the head nigga in charge of affairs". We have a nation full of natural born leaders, that are too damn proud to follow! Everybody trying to school one another, while ain't nobody learning nothing!

Well, this is truly a shame, but it is understandable. It is understandable because we are a people of eternal greatness. We have a lot to be envious and jealous of.

The people who are most envious and jealous of us, are the ones who put us in this very situation. Understand that we are naturally a very, very, very, talented and "gifted" people. Our talents and "gifts" span over all aspects of hue-man endeavor. Sometimes we admire each other's "gifts" so much, that we forget that we are all personally gifted ourselves. This is where the problem sets in.

As an example let us use our imaginations. Let us imagine that we still celebrate that illegal perpetration of a holiday called "Christmas".

Imagine that we were all children. Imagine that, we were all a big family, in the house of God. Imagine that we were all the sons and daughters of God, The Creator. Imagine that God was our direct Father. Do you have the picture yet? Good! I'm sure that you are use to "make-believe" things.

Well, imagine that on "Christmas" morning, that God, our Father, gave us all wonderful "gifts"! Each one of us had a "gift" from God, all to ourselves. Everybody had an individual "gift" under the Christmas tree.

Now as you can imagine, our family is very large, so there are millions of us children running everywhere trying to find our particular "gift". Everybody is excited, but there is one problem. Some of us are finding our "gifts" before others are finding their own "gifts". This is causing a problem.

One child finds his or her "gift", and opens it up to show everybody in the room. Everybody comes over to admire the "gift". Some children come over to admire the other child's God given "gift", and then peacefully go back to search for their own "gift" to open. But other children become impatient and frustrated in searching for their own individual God given "gift", and start to become jealous and envious of the child who has already found their particular "gift".

And out of this jealousy and envy, they become filled with the rage and the evil inspiration to destroy the other child's "gift", while totally ignoring the fact that God has given everyone in the family a "gift", including themselves. This must sound very familiar to you, because it sounds very familiar to me.

And even among the children who have long ago already found and opened their God given "gifts", resentment and devilishment arises within them too. This happens when the devil comes over to visit the house. The devil comes in with and attitude problem deep within his own sick heart. The devil comes over, and he is already upset because he does not ever get a "gift" from God, because of his evil devilishment. So, now he wants to spoil the fun for everybody else.

Once the devil slides his way into the house, by fakin like he is a lil' lamb or a lil' angel of God, he walks over to the children and finds one of them to be his temporary friend. The devil then tells this particular naive little child that his, God given "gift", is better than everyone else's "gifts" by far! Here comes trouble.

The devil then tells the little naive child that he is "too good" to play with the rest of the children. Well, needless to say, eventually the child becomes "big-headed" and conceited. The child has now developed an arrogant attitude, and doesn't even socialize with the family anymore, all because he naively listened to the wicked suggestions of the devil. Is not that a shame? Yes, this is the tricknology of the devil, but the devil isn't finished yet.

Now listen to this. This little wicked devil then seeks out a group of children, aside from the first one he just souped-up. The devil then tells this group of children that the first naive child, thinks that he and his "gift" is better than everybody else in the room. The wicked, deceiving, little, tricky devil then suggests to the group of children, that they should go over there and beat-up the other child and take away his "gift", to teach him a lesson!!!

Well, needless to say, by the end of that day, all of the children are fighting and arguing amongst themselves, while the wicked devil steals everybody's "gifts" and runs back home laughing!!! Meanwhile, God just sits back and lets it all happen, so that we naive little children can learn a big lesson, about entertaining the company of the devil. But obviously we have not learned it yet. We are still full of that...**ENVY, JEALOUSY, AND EGO.**

So yes, we are a very "gifted" people. All of us are "gifted" by The God, in our own individual way. If each one of us is "gifted" in our own way, by God, why should we waste our time being jealous of someone else's "gift"???? Spend that time and energy to find your own God given "gift"!

Don't envy someone else's "gift" when you already have one yourself. The God did not forget you! You just forgot yourself and you forgot The God. You are too busy looking at everybody else's "gift"! Just like a little small minded mischievous little child! Yes, this is you! Yes, this is us!

And, for those of you who have already found your God given "gift", why do you still envy your sister or brother? Why are you still upset with them? You are jealous because they are using their God given "gift" to their advantage. You sittin around huffin and puffin, even though you have a "gift" also. But your brother or your sister ain't lazy like you, so they use their "gifts" wisely. They spend the riches that The God has given them, wisely and efficiently.

What are you doing with what God gave you? Yea, I thought

so. So don't try to pull your successful brother or sister down! Just, learn from them so that you may be successful in utilizing your God given "gifts" too!

Accept your **"own"** God given gifts, and be what The God created **"you"** to be. The God did not skip over you! You skipped over yourself, while worrying about somebody else! Let us kill our foolishness now!

ENVY, JEALOUSY, AND THIS PETTY EGOTISTICAL MADNESS HAS GOT TO DIE!!! Everybody can not be the leader, somebody has to follow! Let the wisdom, truth, and righteousness of The Creator be the leader, and we can all unite and follow together!!!!

Yes, we are all gods and goddesses, but we are still children of the most high God. Everybody has a valuable contribution to the whole, in their own individual way. Everybody is a piece of the larger puzzle. But our own individual piece will never fit, if we don't accept our own and be ourselves! We must accept our own "gift", and be the divine attribute of The God that we are assigned to be, which is ourselves.

Peace

EXPOSING
SEXISM!

My brothers, my brothers, my brothers, my brothers. We need to talk with one another. We really need to have some down to earth, un-cut, straight-talk, with one another. We truly need to address this issue of "Sexism" within our black community. This has become an overwhelming problem in our communities world-wide.

This "Sexism" is eating away at the potential strength of our black communities. This mental illness has set up infection in the brains of the Blackman and is spreading like cancer, throughout our population. This has to be stopped. This has to be stopped by you and by me. This mental illness does not belong to us at all. We picked-up this virus from this whiteman's disease infested mind. This mentality is not ours.

We come from a history of Black gods **and Black goddesses**. We come from a history of Black kings **and Black queens**. We were always together and never apart, until the devil and his way of thinking covered the earth. The Blackman and Blackwoman have always been two halves of one solid strong unit, until we allowed this devil damned mentality to divide and conquer us into these un-unified dis-functional parts. United we stood, but divided we fell.

Blackman we must purify ourselves of this devil's mentality. We must kill that devil within us whenever it comes out. We must slay the devil wherever we find him, even if he is right under our nose. You must kill the devil within yourself. God kills the evil devil no matter where the devil is found. So, if the devil is you, don't expect anything less than a justified execution from The God.

The righteous God of truth will kill the devil, regardless of race, religion, sex or nationality. So, in other words if you sick minded male chauvinist niggas don't kill that devil off that is in you, the Black God will just kill you!!! Plain and simple!

This damn "Sexism" ain't no different than this damn "Racism"! They are both mental illnesses that live in the hearts and minds of devils! All of you weak-minded, egotistical, insecure devils, are truly just punks at the core of your hearts! A racist devil and a sexist devil are really no different from one another, and they all will eventually be cleansed or killed by the righteous Black God, who is a destroyer of the wicked!!! This is your destiny and doom! This is your destiny and doom, if you do not kill off that cancerous mentality immediately!

You think that you are a man because you can "physically" dominate over a woman! But, when it comes to "mental" domination, you become so afraid that you have to start talking all of this male chauvinism talk! You are a punk, and not a man, and I will prove it.

You are actually "weak", because you are just like that weak-ass whiteman that is giving you so much hell! What goes around comes around. The whiteman is constantly trying to hold the Blackman back because he is totally afraid of competing with the Blackman fairly and squarely.

Out of his fear of the Blackman, he seeks to oppress and dominate the Blackman. He seeks to control the Blackman. But if the whiteman was not such a weak-minded, egotistical, punk by nature, he would openly compete with the Blackman fairly and squarely. So he is actually no man at all! He is actually just a soft, weak, insecure punk, working out of fear!

Well Blackman, so it is the same with you, when you exercise a sexist mentality. You want to appear like a man, but your sexist mentality is fueled out of the pure fear of the strength of the Blackwoman!

You are just a pure punk who is afraid to allow the Blackwoman to grow and develop into her full potential!!! You are just afraid that she may develop to be more of a "man" than your weak ass!!! Yes this is true! Yes this is you! Yes this is us! This is a man speaking to a man, and I am man enough to correct my mistakes how about you???

Why are you so afraid of a real Blackwoman? A real Blackman will celebrate and uphold a real Blackwoman. A real Blackman is not afraid of a real Blackwoman! He respects her, he honors her, and would have her no other way!

A real Blackman wants nothing other than a real Blackwoman! A real Blackman don't want no weak, watered-down, overly-submissive, non-opinionated, non-intelligent, non-thinking, over-emotional, "blonde-bimbo" type of woman!!! What in the hell can I do with a woman like this?

What in the hell can you do with a woman like this? You can't do a damn thing with a weak woman like this! This is the type of weak woman that the whitewoman has been made into! A real Blackman don't want no woman like this! Only a weak punk would desire a weak woman like this, so that he could control and dominate over her just to appear strong!

A real Blackman don't want this brain-less dead-weight lingering around him. He wants to be in the company of intelligence and strength! An intelligent and strong Blackwoman will nurture you into an intelligent and strong Blackman if you allow her to, by getting off of your ego! A punk-woman make a punk-man! And I don't want no punk-woman nursing my children with no punk-milk!!!!

Don't take on the mind-set of your oppressor, lest you receive the same doom and destruction that is due to him! You don't want no weak, submissive, un-intelligent, non-thinking Blackwoman, because she will produce weak, submissive, un-intelligent, non-thinking, Black children!!!

A weak Blackwoman will give birth to a weak Black Nation! That is why a true, real, and wise Blackman will not settle for anything less than a 100-percent, 100-proof, absolutely pure, and absolutely powerful strong minded Blackwoman with no bimbo-like characteristics attached!!!

A real Blackman will place his Blackwoman on an elevated pedestal and help her develop in any and every way that is possible, because out of her comes us!! **If she is weak, we are weak!!! If she is strong, we are strong!!**

And as for my beautiful, strong, powerful, Black sisters, I want to talk to you also. I need to talk with you too. I hope that you have been paying attention too! You should know that no true Blackman wants a Blackwoman who is brain-less, thought-less, and weak! This is undesired by the wise righteous true Blackman.

You should not allow yourself to take on any of these weak characteristics! A lot of women have used this male chauvinism, as an excuse to lazily sit back and not do a damn thing! They do not want to develop their own potential, and just want to live off of a man like a parasite!!!

Well you ain't nothing but a damn devil too, because your motivation and inspiration is just as wicked as your egotistical male-chauvinist husband, that is oppressing your silly self! You just want somebody to take care of your big-old over-grown ass! This ain't no damn welfare program! You should not even allow yourself to waste away like that! You have all of that un-explored and un-used brain potential. You should not even allow that to occur.

A real Blackwoman would not even compromise herself to a wicked Blackman. You should not even settle for less than what you deserve! A wicked man will only do to you what you allow him to do to you.

Now back to my black brothers. I want you to understand that this is no attempt to take away your natural manhood. You were born with testosterone and a natural aggressive nature as a leader. But you can not mis-use your nature. Being a man doesn't mean dominating over something or somebody. Being a man means being an effective, righteous, wise, hand of leadership and guidance, to serve the needs of your family. You are a "servant" to your family.

But you can't force your leadership fool! You have to grow in responsibleness, knowledge, and wisdom, and then your family will naturally seek you for guidance and leadership. Ain't nobody going to follow no fool unless they are fools themselves! If you have to force your rule or leadership, then you are obviously doing something wrong!

A true righteous Blackwoman will allow a true righteous Blackman to lead the family with no problems, but if that Blackman is a fool, she will not allow it. A true Blackwoman will let a man be a man, but the man <u>has to be "a man"</u> first!!!

That man can't be no fool. Only a fool has to force his leadership, because don't nobody want to comply with his foolish self. But a righteous man can be a leader without force, because his family can see that he has wisdom and guidance in his head. If you are a <u>righteous Blackman</u>, your family will follow your guidance on their own <u>righteous will</u>.

Now, I know that the whiteman has educated our black sisters and has allowed them to have jobs in white corporate AmeriKKKa, while leaving us Blackmen out the picture. The whiteman did this to attack our "egos" as Blackmen. But if we do not have any "ego" problems, then there is nothing for the whiteman to attack.

He wants us to feel less than men, because we are not making enough money to support our families. He is trying to cause tension and jealousy between the Blackman and Blackwoman, so that we will be divided and conquered by his wicked manipulations. We can't allow this to occur. We must be wise.

Don't become jealous of the Blackwoman. Come down off of your egotistical high-horse and let that Blackwoman give you the education that she has received. We can learn from her, if we swallow this little weak pride. Let your sister give you something to truly be "proud" about. Save the money that she makes from the whiteman's job, and you two start a family business together! We as men, got to stop being so damn proud and start being wise.

Don't let the Blackman and Blackwoman be divided and conquered by the tricknology of this devil, using your own inflated ego to control you and your destiny. Being a sexist devil is just as weak and wicked, as being a racist devil! We got to cleanse ourselves of that mental illness!

We must **<u>embrace</u>, <u>protect</u>, <u>elevate</u>, <u>educate</u>, <u>motivate</u>, <u>uplift</u>, <u>celebrate</u>, <u>respect</u>, <u>honor</u>,** and most of all **"<u>love</u>"** our strong, beautiful, peaceful, and powerful **Black-women-goddesses** in **righteousness!!!** And she will do the same in return, for us. <u>**We shall reign again, forever and ever, but we shall reign together.**</u>

Peace

SOUL-FOOD?
OR
SLAVE-FOOD?
(PART ONE)

Hey listen. I got a whole lot of "soul", but I don't want no greasy, stanky, nasty, disgusting, filthy, funky, pork-guts, most commonly known as "chit-lins"!!! I don't want no pig-snoot, pig-feet, pig-ears, pig-knuckles, or no pig-cracklins! I don't want any of this so-called "soul-food".

There are some parts of the pig, that I can't even mention, but Blackfolks will fry those up too! Hot-sauce will make anything taste good! We eat a lot of this low-quality, low-end, last-resort type of food. We have been eating like this for generations upon generations, but for what reason? We are eating this very low-quality food, while our health is paying a very high price.

Many of us have been raised on this same so-called "soul-food", that is lowering us into the ground before our time, one by one. This so-called "soul-food" diet can be linked to most of our physical, and therefore mental illnesses, dis-eases, and dis-comforts. We are dying from health conditions that cause everything from hypertension, heart-attacks, and strokes, to various forms of cancer. This is directly linked to the poor quality of foods that we have been trained to consume since our birth.

We must clearly understand that this so-called "soul-food"

diet, that has been passed down generation after generation, is actually a "**slave-food**" diet. This poor, low-quality, dis-ease plaguing, suicidal type of diet is the eating habit that we have inherited from that slave plantation. This is not "soul-food"! This is "slave-food"! This food will lay your soul to rest.

This is straight "slave-food", no matter how you look at it. This is the "left-over" scraps that the white slave-master would throw away. The white slave-master would take the nutritional food for himself and the farm animals, and throw away the left over waste material to the niggas and the hogs. The poor, hungry, worked-to-death slave (that's us) would have to go behind the white slavemaster, and dig into the trash to luckily find something similar to food to eat for himself and family.

We would take the trashed scraps of the white slavemaster, and make tasty, but unhealthy meals out of it. We would creatively take these undesired trash scraps, and make them into desired meals by seasoning and cooking them to taste. We would work so much "Black magic" on that so-called food, that the slave master would smell it cooking, and come down to the slave-shack to get some for his own greedy devil self.

Yes, we would miraculously take food, that was only qualitative enough to feed the hogs, and work wonders on it. This so-called food is all that the white slave master had left for us to eat, so we ate it. Even though this food was extremely bad for our Black bodies and Black minds, we ate what we had to eat for Black survival.

So, after eating this type of terrible diet for centuries, during slavery, it became a suicidal habit. This became the only way of eating that we knew. So, this type of food became our trade mark, and it was called "soul-food."

But this was really in fact "slave-food." We have passed on

this style of cooking and style of eating to generation after generation. We have passed on the poor eating habits of slavery on to the present generations. We cooked the "slave-food" so well, that we acquired a taste for it. But, at that time, we had no choice except to eat that "slave-slop" mess. So now that we have a choice, why do we still eat this low quality slave-food that is killing us off mentally as well as physically?

Black people, stop acting a fool for a second and take a look around you! Put down the 40 oz. of brew, for a second, and take a look around you! Wipe that "chit-lin" juice off from around you mouth, for a second, and take a look around you! Stop sucking on that "crack-pipe," for a second, and take a look around you! Stop making that collard-greens and ham-hock sandwich, for a second, and take a look around you! Can't you see what's going on all around you?

Look at all these funeral caravans rollin through our neighborhoods. These coffins are not only carrying the precious Black bodies of the young black men who were gunned-down by nigga-hating niggas! These coffins are carrying the disease infested bodies of the older generations, whose Black bodies are clogged and constipated with the crap of this "slave-food" diet. Their bowels are packed with years of swallowed, undigested, decaying pieces, and chunks of dead pig flesh!!! ...along with every other dead rotting carcass that they could smother in hot sauce!!! Their veins and arteries are clogged with waste that can't find an open passage way out of the body!

Heart attacks, diabetes, cancer, and strokes are eating away at our population. **Death is eating us, because we are eating death.** The more we eat of it, the more it eats of us. You are what you eat. "As a man eateth in his stomach, so is he." If you eat death, you become death. If you eat life, you become life. Think on that.

Take care of your body and be careful about what you put into it. Don't take what I'm saying for a joke. If you want to live, take care of the one physical vessel that you were given. And do not tell me that you can not do it! Stop trying to lie to me and stop lying to yourself. The only fool that you will fool is yourself!

You can take better care of yourself, and you can be more disciplined with your eating habits! Yes you can, because you do it with your cars and trucks, don't you? Yes you do! You take better care of your material possessions than you do of your own material body. Some of you will only put the highest quality of gasoline and oil into your automobiles, but you will put damn near anything of any quality into your own mouth! This is the truth.

You have been taught to love your material possessions more than you love your own self. So as a result of this, you will polish and wax the body of your car all day long in the hot sun, but you yourself are out in public with some old dirty sweat-clothes on your own body and in need of a serious bath yourself.

And after that, you will fire-up a cigarette and open a bottle of malt liquor to kill off your own body, while at the same time, you will kill-off anybody who may accidentally just "scratch" the body of your car. This is the truth. But most of all, this is a shame.

I'm tired of going in circles with this point, because you know this already anyway. Right? Well since you know so much, do your own self a favor. Stop stuffing this slave-slop down your throat. Respect yourself Blackman and Blackwoman. Study to find out what real "soul food" is. **A healthy Black Soul is useless, if it has no healthy Black Body to live in.**

Peace, Love and Respect, **Black.**

TRUE
BLACKMAN

A true Blackman. A real Blackman. A true Blackman is an "alive" Blackman. A true Blackman is an "awakened" Blackman. A true Blackman is a "quickened" Blackman. A true Blackman is an "upright" Blackman. So, who are we? Who are we?

To put it straight and honestly, we are the dead, rotting, remaining, left-over, carcass of the "true" Blackman. I am man enough to admit the truth of the actual fact. We are the remains of what once was a "true" Blackman. We are the dry bones in the valley and the carcass where the eagles have gathered to feast upon our remaining Black flesh. This is us.

Almost everyone on this planet has feasted from the flesh of the Blackman to fill their lusty greedy hungry desire for power, while casting us aside to die.

These pale children thirsted for the **Black power** of their Black Father. They were not patient enough to learn from the Righteous Black Father, so they wickedly sought to take the book away from he who sat at the center upon the throne. So we allowed them to take the book, even though they were not worthy. We allowed the wicked, impatient, immature child to viciously take the book.

In our wisdom, we allowed the child to exercise it's wicked will. This was allowed to teach this child a valuable lesson. The child now has the book, but the child has no understanding of the book.

This child boasts in his "possession" of the book, which directly verifies his childish ignorance to the book.

And so now he wants to imitate his wise Black father. The child now attempts to guide the evolutions of the worlds, with the book in his hand. But his weak and shallow knowledge of the book, prevents his guidance from being effective and righteous. So he is guiding the worlds into doom, destruction and hell. The child could not handle as much as he naively thought he could. So now the Black Father must return to save the worlds, and teach the book. The child must learn to honor thy Black Mother and thy Black Father, that thy days may be longer than six.

But in order to accomplish this goal, of re-claiming the Black throne to teach all 360-degrees of the book, the Black Father must be put back together again. The Black pieces of his torn Black body must be pieced back together to make a brand-new Blackman. Bigger, Better, and Blacker than ever.

This is the re-birth of the Blackman. The Blackwoman will put the pieces of her Blackman back together. This Blackman has been crucified, but this is the day of his resurrection. This Blackman has been crushed to the earth, but out of these smoldering ashes, shall arise a fiery Blackman and Blackwoman that will fly above all levels of present comprehension. The wisdom of this world is exhausted.

It is about time for that naive, impatient, mischievous, little pale child to realize that the "book" is only a sign or symbol to the 360-degrees of knowledge, wisdom, peace and power. The "true" Blackman **is** the "book". The "true" Blackman reigns upon the throne at the center of 360-degrees. The "true" Blackman **is** 360-degrees. The "true" Blackman is the "book".

But right now, we are not the "true" Blackman, as God "created" us to be. We are the "true" Black nigga that the devil "made" us to be. We will not be this way for long. We are waking-up overnight to the knowledge and wisdom of our divine nature. We are learning that we do not belong to the devils, we belong to the all peaceful, all powerful Black God of truth, righteousness, freedom, justice, and equality.

Our Black Father, who art "at" heaven, is master of this day of Judgment and he "maketh us to lay down in green pastures", not the ghetto. And if it is our father who art "at" heaven, then we are the sons and daughters of that God. We are all gods and goddesses, but children of the most high God. The Blackman takes his post within the pyramidal family hierarchy of divine.

No, the Blackman is not the wicked nigga that you think he is. He is not a reflection of the devil by nature, just by circumstance. By nature and under natural circumstances, the "true" Blackman is a perfect reflection of the merciful, beneficent, wise, peaceful, powerful, almighty, illuminated Black God!!! When I say God, I'm not talking about that pale-faced, weak-watered-down, long-haired, enemy-loving, cheek-turning, punkified god, that the devil taught you about! I'm talking about the "true" God and the "true" Blackman!

If you dig deep down into the heart of a devil made nigga, you can find a Blackman. If you dig deep down into the heart of a Blackman, you can find a Black god. If you dig deep down into the heart of a black god, you can find The Black God. So what is a "true" Blackman? Do you still not know? Or is it that you know, but you really don't understand what it is that you think you know?

There is a reason for everything. There is wisdom behind every movement in The Universe. So question everything. Seek and ye shall find the answer, if you are patient and attentive.

Dig down deep within to find the treasure of the "true" Blackman, within yourself. We have to find him, resurrect him, dust him off, shine him up, and let his glorious divine light illuminate the total sphere of the Universe until every other material being is rotating on it's axis in peaceful harmony with the righteous powerful divine laws of creation. The "true" Blackman is now under construction.

Peace Blackman.

TRUE
BLACKWOMAN

A "true" Blackwoman is <u>heaven</u>. A "true" Blackwoman is <u>heaven</u> to a "true" Blackman. A "true" Blackwoman is <u>heaven</u> to the worlds. A "true" Blackwoman is <u>heaven</u>.

She is not the bitch, ho, or slut that this evil world wants to make her. No, she isn't ever going to be that, because she ain't having that! No, not the "true" authentic, real, alive, awakened, Blackwoman. She does not care how corrupt this evil transitory world becomes, she will not yield to it's temptation. Her divine strength does not allow her to compromise to any of the foolishness of her many mischievous children across the globe. This is her, the "true" Blackwoman.

When you see a "black-girl" who is taking on the characteristics of a moral-less bitch, a cheap-ho, or a permiscuous sex-starved slut, she is just that, a "black-girl"! She is no Blackwoman at all, and she is most definitely not even close to a "true" Blackwoman. That is a mentally-dead "black-girl", who is a victim to the evils of this world. She needs to be resurrected into the sphere of her natural divine inner and outer glowing beauty of ancient wisdom. She needs to be her self.

The majestic Blackwoman of truth, is a righteous Blackwoman of the highest morals and discipline. She <u>is</u> the definition of high-esteem. She stands tall with her head in the heavens, and wrapped in the light of the sun giving strength to all of the righteous ones, who are blessed with her steady illuminated presence. She is a fountain of supreme knowledge, wisdom, and intelligence. These are a few characteristics of the "true" Blackwoman.

She is the backbone of strength that has sustained the life of our Black Nation through our "hellfire" of history in AmeriKKKa. She has had to endure much, and she continues to endure much. Our survival would not have been possible if it were not for our strong Blackwoman. She has been the bridge to get us over. This is her.

She has had to take over as "King" as well as Queen, because her "true" Blackman has been viciously murdered and torn to pieces! She has had to endure this hell without the assistance of her "true" Blackman because he is dead. He has been killed. He is not alive in the "true" sense at all. She has endured many days all alone, with no "true" Blackman. She is alone. This is her.

Yes, she searches near and far for the "true" Blackman, but he can not be found. So now the beneficent and merciful God is going to put the pieces of her slain Blackman back together, and make a new "true" Blackman for the "true" Blackwoman and she will never be alone again. So hold on Blackwoman, because when The God finishes making this new "true" Blackman for you, we will be all yours, and you will be all ours! The "true" Blackman and the "true" Blackwoman will be reunited again!

The Blackwoman is not to be disrespected by anyone at anytime. She is not even to be disrespected by her own self, in the least. This is the **QUEEN-MOTHER-GODDESS of the planet Earth and therefore of the Universe.**

She is the sacred holy place of divine creation. Her womb, of "triple divine darkness", is a direct reflection and microcosm to the expanse of the universe where the whole of creation was created.

Her womb is the birthplace of gods and goddesses.

In the triple divine darkness of her fertile womb is the material wealth of all creation. Seven stages of self-creation are all completed here, in the Blackwoman. The Black Womb-of-Man. The Blackwoman. The "true" Blackwoman.

Peace Blackwoman.

"WEAKNESS MUST BE MANIFESTED BEFORE IT CAN BE PERFECTED"

All of the weaknesses of our character must be manifested before the strength of our character can be perfected. But can "you" stand within the light of truth? Can your false pride and shallow ego, endure the exposure, given by the light of truth? Are you emotionally prepared to walk towards the light of truth? Can you really walk the illuminated path of righteousness? Can you really withstand the process of purification?

If we are planning to journey towards the gleaming light of truth, those are very basic questions that we need to ask ourselves, before we begin our journey. We need to ask these basic questions about our journey, so that we will know how to prepare for our journey. We need to know how to carry ourselves and what to bring with us on our journey.

We do not want to bring any unnecessary excess luggage, that may eventually weigh us down. That unnecessary excess weight may slow us down and prevent us from ascending to our ultimate destination. We must take only what is beneficial. We must take only what is necessary to our survival, or we may fall short of our objective and goal. We will just sit there stagnated, while watching our other brothers and sisters "grow-on" past us. You can not ascend towards the spiritual light of truth, if you allow yourself to be weighed down by the heaviness of this material world. So leave your unnecessary excess luggage behind you, or else it will be exposed, by the light of truth, on down the path.

The light of truth shows you the clear-cut reality of things beyond the "shadow" of a doubt. The light of truth cast no "shadows" of doubt, in which things can be hidden. All is revealed. There are no "shadows" because this spiritual light of truth will shine before you, behind you, and all around you. There are no "shadows". The clear-cut reality of things are blatantly shown, revealed, and exposed beyond the "shadow" of any doubt.

Now the main question is, are we sure that we are ready to see the reality of "<u>all</u>" things? Sure we are ready to see the reality of "<u>some</u>" things, but are we really ready to see the reality of "<u>all</u>" things? It is fairly easy to expose something else by the light of truth, but can we withstand to be exposed by the light of truth ourselves? Can your weak ego endure this total exposure? Can your weak pride withstand this total exposure?

The total truth will allow you to see the reality of all things including yourself! Total truth will show you things as they "actually" are, including yourself! Are you sure that you are ready to see things as they "actually" are, including yourself?

Well after total exposure, you may not really be all that you thought you were. While you were putting on that front-show for everybody else, you may have started to believe the hype too! Blatant truth will make you see yourself for who and what you truly are. True knowledge of your true self. You will be exposed. You will truly be exposed.

So, if the truth hurts, can you take the pain? It only hurts for a split second, but if you are resistant to the truth, it can and will hurt forever! Just like getting a shot of medicine with a needle, it will hurt for a split second and eventually heal. But if you tense up to resist it, it will hurt forever. The pain will carry on and on.

So if the truth hurts, will you resist it? Can you take it ? Will you run from the light of truth? Are you afraid of the light of truth? Why should you be afraid? Only a liar will run from the truth! Only a hypocrite is afraid of the truth! The truth is the light!

The truth is the light. The truth is the light that will expose what you hide, as well as illuminate what you manifest. As we walk towards the spiritual light of truth, we are walking away from the materialistic shadow of darkness.

Shadows are cast by material objects that are obstructing the path of light. This unnecessary material weight, that you carry, will reflect the shadows of your doubt. You can not hide your doubts.

You can not hide your doubts of the very things that you claim to believe. In the shadow of darkness, we were able to hide many things and we could hide them from others, as well as ourselves. If we do not see it, then it is out of our sight and therefore out of our minds. Out of sight, out of mind.

Now, in the ignorance of darkness, you could hide a lot of things, but in the light of truth, all that you attempt to hide will be made manifest. You will see all of your own weak points! You will see all of your own hypocrisy! You will see all of your own faults! You will see all of your own contradictions! You will see all of your own weaknesses, beyond the shadow of a doubt. You will be exposed!

But, not only will you be exposed to yourself, you will be exposed to all of those around you. But not only will you be exposed to them, they will all be exposed to you as well. You will all be exposed to one another. This is how it is supposed to be. This is a part of the process.

When Adam and Eve ate of the fruit, or knowledge, their eyes became opened, and they became exposed to one another. Well, if you eat of the knowledge of truth, you will be exposed too! We will be exposed too!

So, cover your ignorance or your nakedness, with the spiritual knowledge and wisdom of your ancient ancestors. Don't keep running and dodging the light of truth. You can not run forever. Where will you run when the clock finally strikes twelve noon? The sun-light of truth will be directly overhead, casting no shadows left nor right in which you can hide your own nakedness or hypocrisy.

At twelve noon, the sun-light of truth is complete, and is exposing to you all, that the darkness of the night time, has kept hidden from your sight. The coming of the sun is drawing near to complete. The sun that you have been praying for! You said that the sun would be coming in the clouds of heaven to save you. The "sun" of man. The "light" of man. The "truth" of man. You shall know the truth and the truth shall make you free.

So, when the sun has completely arrived, do not fear the intense light of the truth. Walk therein! You are the children of the sun. You should fear nothing! You should fear nothing, unless you are trying to hold on to the excess baggage from the weight of this evil world. Lay the excess baggage aside. You can not come with that! You are already stained and soiled enough, with the filth and the dirt of this evil world. It will be task enough to cleanse you of those impurities alone, without you bringing a bag full of filth and dirt weighing you down from your previous worthless life.

This is a brand new day, so you will have to be thoroughly cleansed of yesterday. Do not fear the light of truth because it will cleanse you, if you willingly walk therein. The closer that you walk towards the light of truth, the more and more that our faults will be exposed by the light of truth to everybody within the light of truth. You will gradually see more and more dirt and filth on you than ever before, but don't fear this light. <u>Walk therein</u>! Don't try to turn around and go backwards toward the darkness again, so that you can hide your impurities! Don't feel ashamed. Don't let your false pride manifest. <u>Walk therein</u>! <u>Walk therein</u>!

<u>Walk therein</u>, so that your impurities may be burned away, by the intense heat and light of truth. This way you will have nothing to hide. This light of truth is made-up of "<u>pure-fire</u>". So, allow this truth to be your "<u>purifier</u>". Let this light of truth burn all of your impurities away! <u>Walk therein</u>! That is the only way! You can not be "purified" if you run from the heat of the fire. You can not be "purified" if you hide from the light of the sun/son. Don't be afraid of the sun/son. You are of the son/sun! You are of the truth!

When you feel that burning sensation from the fire of truth, don't become alarmed! That is not "you" burning! That is really the <u>mildew, dirt</u>, and <u>impurities</u> of this world burning off of you! That is not the "true-you" burning away. If it starts to feel like you that is burning, then that obviously means that you need to let go of the excess filth that you are trying to hold on to.

You need to let go of that material excess baggage, because you are most definitely gonna get burned if you don't. The closer that you get to truth, the more that your concealed impurities will be revealed and burned away by the "pure-fire", and if you are holding on to those impurities, you will in turn be burned!

That is why I said that we all have to leave the excess baggage behind us, because eventually we will be exposed! If you are hiding something in your back pocket, it eventually will be exposed! Whatever impurity that you are hiding will be heated-up and set on fire by the pure fire, and before you know it, your whole butt will be intensely burning, until you take what you are hiding out of your pocket, expose it, drop it, and let it be burned away! This is how the light of truth works! Truth will make your inner conscience burn away at you for embracing any known falsehood. You will be purified inside out. God ain't no joke! Truth ain't no joke! So stop joking around, because your ignorance is not amusing!

You will be exposed for who you really are. After you willingly go through the "purifier", what is left of you, is the true you. All of the past impurities are burned away! The true you is now exposed. After the "pure-fire", the true you is a beautiful you! A shiny, shimmering, gleamy you! The true you!

You have to burn away the coal to get to the diamond inside. The diamond is you, or the true you. So, do not run from the truth! Don't run from the heat! Don't run from the light! Don't run from the sun! Don't run from the fire, lest you may never dis-cover the true diamond inside... the true you.

Admit your weaknesses openly, and show the rest of the world your strength in overcoming your weaknesses! You will overcome them by going through the "pure-fire". Don't be ashamed of your faults! Don't cry over your spilled milk, nor should you try to hide it. Just mop it up and go on! Mop it up! Don't be so proud that you can't mop up your own mistakes! That is foolish! Don't pretend like you didn't spill something in the first place! Mop it up! If you don't, you will eventually step right into the puddle. Either you will step into it or somebody else will. So, just mop it up and put your pride aside!

Don't run from the problems that plague you! Expose them and then attack them! The doctor can not cure you of your illness, if you are too proud to admit that you are ill. You really are sick, with your ego. How can the mechanic fix it, if you don't tell the mechanic that it is broken? Problems can only be corrected after they are first exposed.

So don't get upset when your <u>problems</u>, <u>weaknesses</u>, <u>short-comings</u>, and <u>faults</u> are exposed by the light of truth. Don't get upset and emotional because you now see yourself for who you really are. Don't get upset. Don't get upset at someone who speaks the truth that exposes your faults and weaknesses. It is not their fault that you are weak. You should thank that person for exposing your problem, because now that you know the problem is there, you can fix it! But had you never been exposed, you would still be carrying that excess baggage around forever, while not knowing what was holding you back all of the time.

Be thankful for the truth! Be thankful for those who speak the truth! Because, only the truth will make you free of your own ignorance. The truth exposes that which you previously were ignorant of, but now you know. Now you know what wrongs must be corrected, thanks to the light of truth.

Attack your problems, not the truth! Attack your faults, not the truth sayers! Attack the weakness in yourself instead of attacking the strength in others beside you. Don't be a crab, trying to pull everybody else down, just because your weak misery loves company.

If you choose to walk the straight and narrow path of truth towards the light, you will be exposed! You should expect to be exposed! You should be thankful to be exposed!!! Do not resist your purification, lest you remain impure! Do not resist the truth, lest you remain in the midst of lies.

The son/sun is rising, but you don't have to run for shelter. You are the children of the son/sun, <u>so walk therein</u>. The son/sun-light is not "your" enemy. The truth is not "your" enemy. Only liars run from the truth, and thieves run from the light. So don't retreat, just repent. Don't retreat, just repent.

Remember the one thing about complete purification. **All of the weaknesses of your character must be made manifested, before the strengths of your character can be made perfected**.

Peace, Strength, and Blessings be with you.

EDUCATION

VS.

CERTIFICATION

We often hear different people "attempt" to offer solutions to the problems that our Black Nation suffers from. And we often hear the same solution repeated. We hear statements like "Our people need education!" or "Education is the key!". Well, these "tired" statements are becoming very useless, purposeless, and just plain played-out!!! But why is this?

Well let us conduct a critical analysis of this subject. Of course, our people need an education! That is obvious, but what do you mean when you say "education"? What does "education" mean to you? Can you explain what an "education" is? What is it that you are talking about? Yes, our people need an education to succeed, but not the type of education that you are talking about, with your brain-washed self.

Well, let us be honest with one another. Whitefolks have let us go to their schools for quite sometime now, to receive a "so-called education". But it seems that we are even more blind, deaf, and dumb now, than we were before they let us in!!! So what's up with that?

I thought that "education" was supposed to enlighten our minds, not oppress, suppress and depress our minds. We come out of this "so-called" educational system more stupified than ever! We lose our common sense! We lose our natural minds! Most of the time we come out even forgetting the fact that we are "Black". We lose our own self-identity.

All of a sudden we become an "American". So, we quickly forget that we have been the victims of "Americans" for over four centuries! Fool, you are not an "American" or else you would not have to fight (or "beg") for the rights of a real white American!!! You are just a victim, or I should say one of the many victims of these true Americans!

You go off to school and don't want to be "Black" anymore. Now you want to be a "Democrat" or "Republican", which are the flip sides of the same coin. Self-Preservation is rule number one, but you don't want to preserve your Black-Self. You want to jump into the great "American melting-pot"; so that you can come out melted-down, watered-down, thinned-out, and just plain weak!

You are such a pitiful sight to see. You are like a strong cup of "Black" coffee with too much "white" cream in it! You used to be strong, but now you just weak! If I could, I would just pour your watered down weak-self down the drain. You are useless to your people. You need to be strong and Black to wake-up your sleeping people.

Now, getting back to the subject matter at hand. Let us continue discussing this "so-called" education. You say that our people need education, but this educational system has been driving our people, especially our children, further into the grave of mental ignorance.

Our children come out of the womb as inquisitive and intelligent as children can come. As toddlers, our children show brilliance in social comprehension, and physical coordination skills. When our children start to speak, they make most adults feel extremely stupid. The children come out of the womb as natural born critical thinkers. They ask you questions that you can't even begin to answer, and they give you simplified suggested solutions to the problems that you can't seem to figure out.

Yes, our children are naturally intelligent, but what happens to them before they become adults? Once our children enter this school system, they lose all signs of the "Black Brilliance" that they were naturally born with.

Around the fourth and fifth grade, they become totally un-interested in learning. Their natural inspiration and motivation is abruptly snuffed-out by this, slow-moving, non-relevant, inaccurate, non-functional, un-inspirational, poor excuse for an educational school system! Our children are being mentally murdered in the so-called educational system of AmeriKKKa!!!

We send our children to whitefolks, and wonder why they come back so poorly educated! We leave the education of our precious young Black minds, to the discretion of our former slave masters! This is our own mental suicide! Do you really think that these people are all of a sudden interested in cultivating a young Black mind to full potential? Hell No! Hell No!

After they worked night and day for centuries to destroy the greatness of the Black mind, they are not going to do a 180 degrees turn-around! This is against their nature! This would be to their own dis-advantage. Why would they work to cultivate our young Black minds to full development, just so that we could rise up and take them out of power?

Don't you know that their whole reason for being racist towards you is because of their deep-seeded jealousy of you? That is why you will find the most racist of whitefolks trying to lay out in the sun to get darker, but they are getting nothing but cancer. Dumb devils. But they are not dumb enough to fully educate your children, and you are dumb enough to expect them to!

When your child comes home wondering what is wrong with his or her wide nose, kinky hair, and thick lips, don't look puzzled! Don't wonder why your child starts talking all funny, as if they have a nasal problem! Don't wonder why they want to bleach their hair and skin! Don't wonder why they keep bringing home little white boys or girls as their dates! Don't wonder why your child has an inferiority complex about being Black!

That damn school curriculum is teaching "subliminal" white superiority! And if you were not so mentally blind, you would see that it is really "blatant" white superiority! Your children are not being educated, they are being annihilated!!!

Your children can not learn anything else "effectively", until they first learn the knowledge of self. This goes for you too! You can not effectively learn anything else until you first have a true knowledge of your true self. You can't build a pyramid of knowledge until you first build a firm and solid foundation. That first foundation is yourself. But the reason that our educational building blocks fall down is because we don't truly know our true selves. We have no foundation. We have no base. You must understand the process of learning, to truly understand why we fail.

The process of learning begins very, very, very, very early in our lives, as soon as we are introduced to the material universe. We began to compare everything around us in relation to our own selves.

The way that you obtain information or knowledge is through

perception. The way that you perceive things, is to perceive them in comparison to yourself, for proper understanding. But, before you gather information to compare to your own self, you must first properly perceive and understand your own self, in order to properly perceive and understand what is outside of your own self.

Then, as you grow in accumulative information, knowledge, or data, you compare the new information to the accumulated knowledge that you already have, in order to gain a proper understanding of what you are now attempting to perceive.

To gain a proper and thorough understanding of something, it must be made relevant to your own personal self. This means that if one has no true knowledge of their true self, they can not truly perceive anything outside of themselves. The educational process must be made relevant to us, to be effective. Do you understand what I'm saying? Do you really understand?

Your children, and you too, must learn every aspect of our true selves. We must learn our <u>true</u> history. The reason why we don't know what's going on now and where in this hell we are going, is because we don't know where in this hell we have been! We don't know our <u>true</u> history, so therefore we don't know our true destiny.

I know, that some of you know your so-called "African-American" history, but that is not what I am talking about here. This so-called "African-American" history, that white folk are willing to teach you now, is a great history, but we must realize one thing. This so-called "African-American" history is the record of our great achievements as physical and mental slaves.

This is our history after the destruction of Black Greatness. This is our history as courageous slaves, who performed amazing accomplishments under the oppression and suppression of the most notorious, wicked, criminal government ever assembled in world history. So if we can exhibit such "genius" in mental and physical chains, just imagine the genius that we could exhibit if we were truly totally free!

This is why "intelligent" white folk know that they must maintain a psychological system of tricknology to keep you down, so that they can maintain their power over the world!!!

As for "un-intelligent" whitefolk, like red-neck, tobacco-chewing, pick-up truck driving whitefolks; they are racists, because they are just plain stupid!!! They don't live in any better conditions than poor Black people, but they still got the nerve to think of you as a "nigger." These fools don't realize that they are nothing but "white-niggers", according to their own upper-class white brethren.

These days, your white skin can't even save you from the evils of this wicked government. It is written in the books of scripture that, in the last days, satan shall cast out satan.

Let us get back to the point. Black people, understand that you were not slaves since the beginning of time. Please study your great ancient history "before" you were slaves. You were not always slaves. You were exhibiting your genius, mastery, and greatness, before the caucasian race was introduced to the light of the sun!!! You are The Original People of the earth, so therefore, you have a long legacy of historical greatness that has been unsurpassed to this date.

Your historical ancient greatness, makes your achievements as "African-Americans", look like child's play. Your ancient historical greatness makes european or caucasian historical achievements look very minimal as well. Don't ever forget that we are the direct descendants of Kings, Queens, Gods, and Goddesses.

So, this means that this great potential for universal

greatness is written inside of the genetic coding of your physical existence and being. All of this historical legacy of 360 degrees of divine scientific excellence is recorded within your DNA. We, as The Original People of the earth, do not pour knowledge into "our" minds, we extract knowledge and wisdom from within "our" minds. We use books and other external resources as "stimuli", to bring the wisdom up and out from our subconscious minds. This is true.

This is the ancient "African" method of educating. The African demanded that the student exercise and develop his or her mind by "intellectualizing" aggressively. Knowledge is pulled out from within, for the African. This, of course, is quite contrary to the method of the european caucasian ideology and application of education.

The european caucasian uses the method of **"memorization"**, not. **"intellectualization"**. The european caucasian demands that their students "memorize" the information given by the instructor. Then the student must recite what they have "memorized" to prove themselves intellectually. Of course, this method is stupid, and it is trying to stupify the student as well .

Just because the student has "memorized" information, doesn't indicate that the student has developed the ability to think, intellectualize, contemplate, or mentally problem solve. This "memorization" is not mind-development; it is mind programming. This memorization doesn't train a person to use their mind as a productive tool at all, it just uses the mind as a dysfunctional empty bucket to hold irrelevant information.

You can memorize all of the information and data in the world, but that doesn't mean that you have the common sense skills needed to effectively use your memorized knowledge, for problem solving or "intellectualizing". "Memorization" does not exercise your mind for thinking. While, "intellectualization" vigorously exercises your mental thinking abilities.

This intellectualization is the educational method used by our ancestors. We would constantly ask effective critical questions, and then contemplate effective critical answers. Our teachers would not directly give us the answers to our many questions, but we were challenged to search for the answers ourselves. This gives the mind its strength. This is the method of supreme education.

The teacher doesn't give you answers, to "memorize". Instead the teacher gives you questions upon which to "intellectualize". If a mind has the ability to come up with a question, it also has the ability to answer the question it produced or conceived. The sum total of potentiality is contained within the 360 degrees of your Black mind. It is just up to you to explore the "inner-space" of your mind to find the concealed treasures. Know thyself and thy shall know the Universe!

The whole key to our proper and effective education, is to internalize our true knowledge of our true selves, but this present form of western education will not do that for us. This whole "educational" system is not about true education at all. This system has nothing to do with "education"! This system is centered around "certification". Did you understand what I just said?

This system has nothing to do with "education". This system is primarily centered around "certification"! This means that all of you who boast and brag about your BA, BS, MA, MS, and PHD "degrees", have been duped! These are not necessarily degrees of higher education! These are "degrees" of higher certification! Yes, you can deny it all that you want to, but the truth is just the truth!

Look at the university or college system in AmeriKKKa, which is actually an incorporated multi-billion dollar industry. Yes, you have paid thousands upon thousands of dollars for your "certification", not your "education". This is true. Let us take an objective look at this thing together.

You know good and well that you have paid all of that money for a simple piece of paper! That piece of paper signifies that you are "certified", not "educated". So you have paid thousands of dollars for a piece of paper. Yes, you should not allow yourself to be fooled.

No, you shouldn't be fooled, because I could walk into your university library today, and sit right next to you and read the same book of information. You are thousands of dollars in the hole, so that you can read the same information that I'm reading for free. And if I can't get into the university library, I can go to the public library. And if they don't have the book, I can make them order the book!

Yes, so you say that I can't sit in the classroom with you for free. Well, you are correct, I can not come to class with you for free. But, I don't need any boring, un-enthusiastic, under-paid, life-less, so-called professor to read a book to me and give me his or her opinions and commentary on the side. You don't need one either. I can read to myself. You can read for yourself. We pay these so-called professors to "grade" us or give their so-called scholarly opinions of us. We pay these people to tell us if we are worth something or not. If they grade you with an "A", you feel good about yourself. If they grade you with an "F", you feel bad about yourself. You pay them for their opinions.

This is true in the most basic sense. They have a so-called "valued-opinion", so you pay thousands of dollars, in valued dollars, for their so-called valued opinions. Their opinion determines whether or not you will be viewed as valuably intelligent or as worthlessly un-intelligent by the world. But wait! Who in this hell cares about their opinions? You do, and your slavemasters do! But why? Well, we will get to that a little later.

Now, I don't want you to think that I am saying that everybody should drop out of school. And I am not saying that all professors have no educational value either. What I am saying is that we must start to think independently. Don't **depend** on the college or university to educate you, because you **will** come up short. If you are going to attend a university or college, take it upon yourself to educate yourself aside from what they give you. Use their resources to the maximum. Live in their libraries. Live in their laboratories. You must encourage yourself and do for self.

I have seen many "dumb" people graduate from universities with so-called "masters" degrees. But what have they mastered? They have mastered the method of memorization. They have mastered the art of taking a test. They think that they have received an education, but in fact they have received nothing but higher certification. People pay big money for these "degrees" and assume that their education is completed. This could not be further from the fact of truth.

They have actually only scratched the surface of basic knowledge. Black people, please don't stop with mere certification. Continue with independent education. Let your mind continue to grow beyond that "basic" education. I call it "basic", because it is the "base" or foundation for your real education. That is why they put a "square" on your head at graduation time. The "square" represents just a mere "base" upon which you should build your pyramid of real education.

So, you thought that you were finished at graduation, when in actuality you were just being prepared. But you are too tired now. This educational process was made to slow you down and drain you of your learning enthusiasm. Now you claim to be too old and too tired to develop your mind. This is all in the plan. This is the intricate sophistication of tricknology used on you. This is to keep you suppressed, oppressed, and depressed. Think on that. Think deeply on that.

So, use and exploit these institutions, just as they use an exploit you! Exhaust their libraries and exhaust their professors! There are some good professors out there so exhaust them! And as for you professors and teachers, remember the first rule of being an educator; **"The best of teachers, never stop being the BEST of students!"** Please remember that statement, and live by it. You will then always be successful.

And, as far you students, remember one thing; even if you have a good teacher, don't spend all of your time just trying to learn what your teacher knows. You are supposed to be aiming far beyond their scope of knowledge. How else are we going to grow in intellect, generation after generation?

Don't learn all that your teacher has to teach, and then get satisfied. That is very foolish! We would be stuck in a repetitive and foolish cycle, if we embraced that unproductive philosophy. Use your teachers as stepping stones, not as goals to reach or as points of destination. We must progress, generation after generation, beyond the achievements of our fore-parents or ancestors.

Now wait a minute, there is another moral to this story. As to my many brothers and sisters, who can not afford to pay the ridiculous prices of colleges and universities, do not despair! Please do not feel as if there is no hope for your education, just because you can't afford to pay for the white man's certification.

My beloved brothers and sisters, you can go to the libraries of AmeriKKKa, and get an education that will far exceed that of any university or college. You could intellectually embarrass most college graduates with the knowledge that you could acquire from inspired independent study!

Look at the example of Malcolm X. My brother destroyed Harvard and Yale university graduates during heated intellectual debates! This is because Malcolm X had the ability to think and exercise his mind quickly, while his weak opponents could only depend upon their memorized bank of information to help them. Malcolm X could think far beyond the scope of his opponents.

These weak opponents could only think within the scope of their professor's knowledge. They could only think within the scope of their accumulated "memorized" knowledge. So, please remember the example that Malcolm X made for us.

Don't use the fact that you have no money as an excuse. The public library is free to you. This knowledge is waiting for you. White people say that the best place to hide something from a Blackman, is to put it in a book. Can you believe that? Well it is true. All of the knowledge and history of your ancestral legacies of greatness is documented. These people study about you, but now you must study about yourself. And after you study that, study everything else.

Reading opens your mind up to whole new worlds! I know that this "reading" stuff sounds all corny, but I'm serious. I, myself, used to hate to read. I hated reading! This is because those whitefolks at school had me reading all of those irrelevant, stupid, boring materials that did not mean a damn thing to me! But, after I read the autobiography of Brother Minister Malcolm X, I couldn't stop reading. I just started reading things that were relevant to me and my existence. This opened up my mind to a whole new level of consciousness.

Do you know what I'm sayin? Do you understand? See, I didn't like reading before, because of what they (whitefolks), were giving me to read. But now I love reading, because I know what my mind hungers for. The mind is like a second stomach. Except, this stomach is for digesting mental food instead of physical food. But, just as physical food is eaten to give physical nourishment to the body, mental food is consumed to give mental nourishment and healthiness to the mind.

Healthiness of the mind is most important, because the mind controls everything else. The mind is the master computer to your very existence. If you feed your mind filth, you will have filthy thoughts. If you feed your mind with healthy food, you will produce healthy thoughts. "Food for thought."

Please continue feeding your mind with healthy food, so that you can maintain a state of mental healthiness. And there is free food at the libraries for you. So after you have fed and satisfied yourself, come back and feed the multitudes of your mentally starved people.

Now let us continue to break down this system of tricknology, under the disguise of a "educational system". This is nothing but a modern-day system of slave certification. Corporate AmeriKKKa is nothing more than a modern slave plantation. It is the same thing, but just more wisely up-graded for modern times.

Instead of pork and grits, you get a little paycheck to take home to your starving family. Instead of crowded slave quarters, they gave you the crowded inner-city housing. Instead of getting beaten for not being a good little "slave-nigga", you get beaten for not being a good little "nigga-slave". Or if you're lucky, you will just get fired from your job and your name will be put-out over the corporate wire as a "troublemaker", so that nobody else will hire you in that city. You are a corporate slave.

Your whole life revolves around your job. You wake up, get ready for work, go to work, watch the clock all day, get off work, come home, eat dinner, get prepared for work the next day, go to sleep, wake up, and start all over again. What in the hell kind of life is that?!?! It's the life of a slave.

You are a corporate slave, and the educational system "certifies" what <u>level of a slave</u> you will be. The educational system and schools are slave training centers that determine what plantation you will eventually serve at. If you have a high school degree, you work in the "fields", and if you have a college degree, you work in the "house".

Yes, that is right back to the "house-nigga" and the "field-nigga". And the "house-nigga" <u>still</u> thinks he is better than that "field-nigga", just because "Massa Harvard" or "Massa Yale" put a gold star on his house-nigga forehead. The gold star says PHD, or whatever type of certified nigga you may be.

<u>Whenever you are laboring or working day and night for the benefit of somebody else's Nation, you are a slave.</u> Even those of you making over $100,000 dollars a year are slaves. If your white boss can afford to pay your black-ass that amount of money, how much do you think he is paying himself, fool?!? If you're getting paid a million, he is making a billion off of your talents and services. Don't be fooled!

Think of what you would make if you were your own boss. All of your talents and services are going toward the sustaining and upliftment of this white nation, but you don't even think about your own Nation. (...by the way, I'm not talking about this ameriKKKan nation or the united nations, I'm talking about your own **Black Nation!!!**)

You living in somebody else's house. And if they decided to

stop giving you an allowance, for your chores, and kicked you out of their house, you would fall flat on your butt. This is us. Modern day slaves dependent upon "massa" for our survival. This is us.

This modern day educational system is a preparatory plantation system. You are trained to think within a certain mind-set. You are made and molded into the image of a "marketable slave". You have to fit the standards that are set-up by the top corporate slave owners of AmeriKKKa. The preparatory plantation (university or college) grade you according to how well you fit the mold. They want to see how well you follow directions, and they want to test your loyalty.

You are trained and trained and tested and tested. They teach you how to memorize, so that you can memorize the directions and orders that will be given to you in corporate slave AmeriKKKa. After your training is completed on the slave-campus, you are stamped with a certain slave-certification.

If you qualify, you may get a chance to serve at some of the top plantations in the country. But if you get a lower grading from your preparatory plantation, you will probably be moving from plantation to plantation throughout your life. You just take the piece of paper, that your "training massa" gave you, and show it to the "massas" at the other plantations. They might let you work at their plantation, if the "training massa" said that you were good enough. This is true. Don't try to deny the truth. This is you. This is me. This is us.

So, all of you house negroes who pride yourselves in the "gold PHD star" that massa gave you, think again. You are just a certified nigga. You are groomed by the white man, trained by the whiteman, and certified by the whiteman, to work for the benefit of the whiteman.

My brothers and sisters, we can't discontinue our education with just the whiteman's certifications. <u>We</u> must enrich <u>our</u> minds beyond the training of the whiteman. He is not going to train us to be smarter than him. Go ahead and get the whiteman's training, and get your own independent education also. But once you get it, don't be foolish enough to work for the benefit of the whiteman. You are helping him to keep his foot on your own back.

Use your knowledge and skills to uplift your own Black Nation. Foreigners travel here, all the time, to get knowledge and skills, but they take it back home for the uplifting of their own people. That is wise. You should be wise too. We should be wise too. You are going to be wise from now on.

Wake up Blackman and Blackwoman! Do for self! Don't be left out in the cold, when these people finally decide to stop giving you and me an allowance. Be a Black Man! Be a Black Woman! Stop being a modern hi-tech slave! When you go to these universities and colleges, understand that you are receiving a certification. Independently seek out your own education.

Any man that controls the mental input of your mind's information, controls the total sphere of your thinking. Don't fall prey to the tricknology. Accept your <u>own</u> and be yourself! <u>Accept</u> - <u>your</u> - <u>own</u> - <u>and</u> - <u>be</u> - <u>yourself</u>!

Think about it.

"HEAVEN, HELL AND JUDGMENT DAYS"

Okay, so let us clear all of this madness up, with a quickness! I'm not even going to insult your intelligence any more than you have already insulted your own intelligence. You know good and well that the fairytale teachings about "Heaven and Hell" given to us by the white slavemaster and "Reverend Collard Greens", is a damn lie!!! You know that is a lie.

Yes, we have been lied to! Brother and Sister we have been raised on falsehood, fairytales, and fictional stories. In other words, we have been constantly lied to every since our date of birth! That is why our minds are so messed-up now! We are trying to live in a realistic, non-fictional world, with a brain that is fueled by imaginary, spooky, hocus-pocus, Walt Disney, fantasy lies! It is no wonder, why we don't know what the hell is going on around us!

Black people please, please, please, stop feeding these damn lies to our precious Black children! Feed these precious young Black minds reality and truth that they may be well equipped to deal with a realistic world! That is why your children grow-up and stop talking to you!!! Why should the child seek advice from somebody that has been lying to them all of their lives??? Huh? Answer that!

Now let us tell some truth to combat some of these lies that have been forced down our throats! First of all, it ain't no such thing as no big, fat, jolly, red-nosed whiteman named Santa Claus, that be sliding his big, fat, flat, white buttocks down nobody's chimney on no so-called Christmas Eve! There ain't no damn chimneys in the ghetto no way!

Second of all, there ain't no hocus-pocus, spookified, flying white woman called the "toothfairy" that's gonna give you some money for your nasty, dried-up, rotted-out tooth laying under your pillow!!! I better not catch no flying whitefolks around my house!

Third of all, there ain't no curly head, little miniature, naked white boy with no white feathered wings on his back that is gonna shoot you on Valentines Day to make you fall in fantasy love with somebody, who never gave you a second look, before this lil' naked chubby whiteboy shot'em in the butt with an arrow!

Yes, we could go on and on talking about the lies that we have been fed, but let us address the specific lies told to us about "Heaven and Hell". We already know that there ain't no white pearly gates, no white streets paved with gold, no flying white angels, and no white God of righteousness. Ain't none of that white madness true! It's a big white lie!!!

We also know that there ain't no bugged-out crazy red-man with a pitch fork, living under the ground giving people all kinds of hell! The real devil is giving you all kinds of hell right here on top of the ground!

There also ain't going to be no "fairytale" Judgment Day, where some hippy looking white boy is going to comeback from the dead with holes in his hands and feet, from 2000 years ago, to raise all of the dead folks out of the cemetery, into the air for a rapture in the sky! How in this hell could we have ever believed this pure foolishness?

All praises are due to the merciful and beneficent God for waging war on our circumstantial, ignorance and naivete. So, let us attempt to study one of the true basic understandings of "Heaven, Hell and Judgment Day(s)". Let's wise up.

Heaven and Hell ain't no two places that you go to after your physical death, necessarily, but they are rather just two different "states of mind", "states of being", "states of existence", and "conditions of life". Heaven and Hell occurs right here on top of this earth. "Paradise" is the "Here-after", but it is "here" - "after" the destruction of this true devil's transitory evil world, or this so-called civilization. Think about it. "...thy kingdom come, thy will be done on earth as it is in heaven." Think about it.

Your mental state determines the outcome of your physical existence. This means that if you have a "hell" state of mind, you will produce a "hell" in every one of your other states of existence. This also means that if you have a "heaven" state of mind, you will produce a "heaven" in every one of your other states of existence. As a man thinketh in his heart, so is he.

Well, the true devil has kidnapped you and I from the "heavens" (multiple heavenly states of existence: mental-heaven, spiritual-heaven, biological-heaven, environmental-heaven, economical-heaven, social-heaven) and delivered us straight to hell, so that he may dwell in our "Heavens". "Whiteman heaven is a Blackman hell".

So this means that, whether you know it or not, we are stuck in the constipated bowels of this whiteman's so-called civilization and this is the "true" hell. This is the true hell and for those who disagree without knowledge, "This sure in the hell ain't heaven!" Right? We will continue this aspect later, in our studies.

Now, let us concentrate and meditate on Heaven and Hell, as

they apply to "conditions of life", which are brought on by "states of mind". Do you understand? Am I being clear? I don't want us to be anymore confused than whitefolks have already confused us!

Let us move on. Being a crack addict is a "mental hell". Being in love is a "mental heaven". Contracting a deadly disease is a "biological hell". Having perfect health is a "biological heaven". Being completely paralyzed can be a "physical hell". Exercising your full athletic potential, is a "physical heaven". The death of a loved one is an "emotional hell". The birth of a new child can be an "emotional heaven".

These are all just different conditions of life that we experience. But how do we maintain more "heavens" during our lives than "hells"? A bunch of "little heavens" make up one "big heaven", and a bunch of "little hells" make one "big hell". But still, how do we produce "heavens" in our lives, instead of "hells".

This is all determined by "Judgment Day(s)". I'm not talking about the big "Judgment Day" that we are obviously going through right now, although all Judgment Days work on the same principles, whether big, small, micro or macro. I'm talking about all of the multiple "Judgment Days" that make up the one big "Judgment Day". They all determine whether or not you receive a condition of hell, or a condition of heaven into your life.

Even though this big Judgment Day is being judged by the almighty God, who is the Master of this day of judgment, the smaller judgment days can be judged by us. We can determine a measure of our fate. We can determine a heaven or a hell for our own selves, depending upon our own judgments, which are actually "decisions".

A judgment is a resolute and absolute decision. We make constant decisions during our everyday lives. We make constant decisions on a conscious basis and on a sub-conscious basis, but nevertheless we are making decisions constantly. These many different decisions are all "Judgment Days" that determine the outcome of heaven or hell into our individual life experiences. Do you understand?

If we make bad decisions on our individual judgment days, we will bring bad conditions of hell into our lives. If we make good decisions on our individual judgment days, we will bring good conditions of heaven into our lives. Do you understand what is being said? Is it being said plainly enough? The devil has made our minds so chaotic with confusion, that we sometimes don't see the truth which is hidden in simplicity. This makes us forsake our own common sense.

Let us move on. How do we have heaven in our lives? "<u>By having a successful Judgment day.</u>" How do we have a successful judgment day? "<u>By making a good judgment or decision</u>". How do we make good judgments or decisions? "<u>By using the right 'resources' upon which to fuel and base our decision or judgment.</u>"

You can not make the proper judgment or decision, without using the proper resources to do so. All of these judgments and decisions are little tests, that could take us to another level or cause us to stay at the same level repeating the same mistakes. This depends on if we pass or fail the test. Just like with any test, you must have the proper resources to study from to gather the correct answers, in order to past your test, by making the right "decisions".

Now within each and every one of us is a rich abundance of "decision-making resources". Inside of our consciousness is every possible resource good and bad.

This is just like the rich earth which is full of resources, whether good or bad. In the earth you can find the natural resources for mass nuclear destruction, or you could find the natural herbal resources for mass medicinal healing. You could produce a physical hell on the earth or you could produce a physical heaven on the earth. This just depends on the righteous or wicked will of the particular mind/person. So, it is the same with the natural mental resources within us all.

Brothers and Sisters, this is a simple but most important subject. If applied, this could bring immediate results into our lives on many different levels. Let us look at the main mental resources that we all contain within our consciousness. Then we can choose which resources are best qualified to fuel and motivate our decisions.

Our resources exist in the form of "levels of consciousness." These are: *(see illustration)*

The Blackman and Blackwoman are both created to contain 360 degrees of the sum total of Potentiality. This means that "all" is contained in the Black. You and I have the potential to manifest all of these different "judgment-resources" or "human-qualities". We have the potential for extreme bad as well as extreme good. Do not ever forget that the devil was produced from the weaker and lower germ of the Original Blackman. The devil is nothing more than your own "lower self" in the person and in the flesh. This is truth.

Your "lower self", in the flesh (whiteman), rules over you, and therefore makes an extreme condition of hell in your life. So it is the same with your own personal "lower self".

The devil, in the flesh, pulls you down by catering to your appetite and emotional levels. He wishes to bring out the worst qualities of the Original Man and Original Woman. By constantly trying to stimulate the "lower-qualities" of the Original Nation, the devil seeks to make us create a perpetual hell for ourselves. This

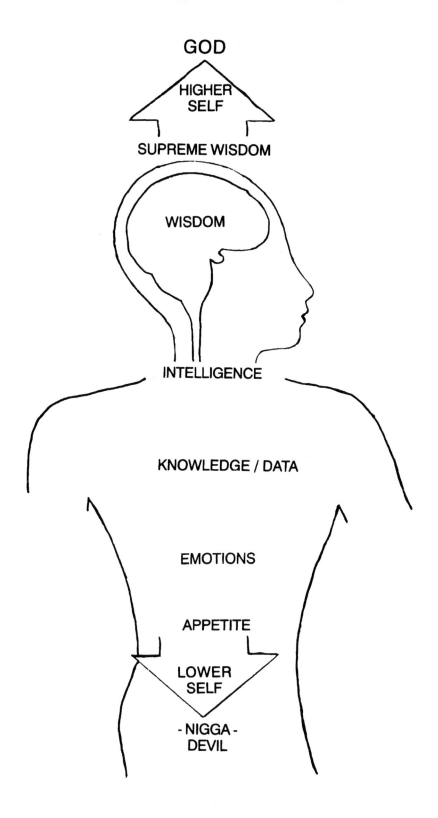

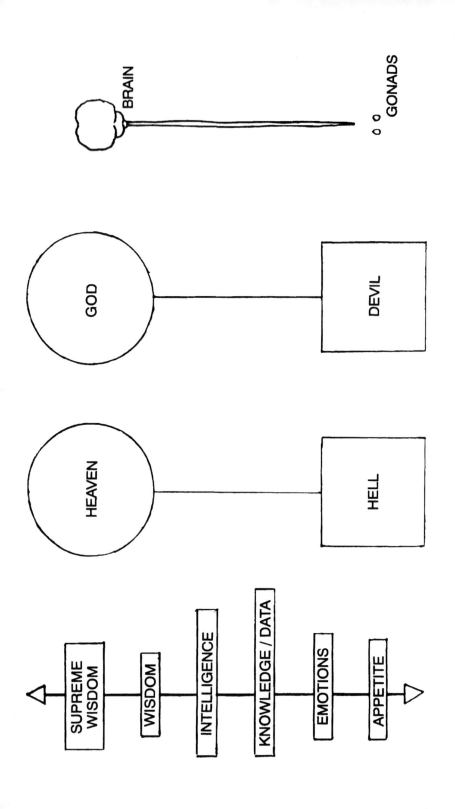

brings us down to the devil's lower level of consciousness. Misery loves company.

Now let us get back to the list of "mental resources" or "levels of consciousness". You have many "Judgment Days" or decisions in your life. You have the natural resources within your levels of consciousness in which to fuel your decisions such as, supreme wisdom, wisdom, intelligence, knowledge/data, logic/reasoning, emotions, and appetite.

All of these qualities inter-act and work together, but they must be <u>controlled</u> and <u>prioritized</u>. We can not allow a "lesser" quality to overtake a "greater" quality. This could lead to big trouble. Their must be a <u>chain of command.</u>

For example if you allow your lower emotions to overtake your higher intelligence, these lower emotions can guide you straight into a serious condition of hell. If you are in a lower emotional frame of mind, this will cause you to make bad decisions during your judgment days.

Let us say that you are manifesting the lower emotion of jealousy, for example. Jealousy has just overtaken all of the intelligence, wisdom and knowledge of your mind! You come home to find your spouse in bed with your best friend! Your "jealousy" is now automatically mixed with a dangerous condition of emotional "anger" too. All of this chemical reaction has taken total control of your mind! Your lower emotional self is calling the shots! But wait, here is a judgment day!

You now have to "judge" or decide how to deal with this unfortunate situation. Now remember that your judgment or decision, directly determines your future of hell or of heaven!

So what do you do about this situation? How will you decide or judge? Well, since your higher self has been overtaken by your lower emotions of "jealousy" and "anger", your judgment will reflect that fact.

So, you and your emotions decide to physically attack and beat-down your so-called best friend. Your so-called spouse, starts screaming at you to stop! So, you do stop the beating, and grab a loaded gun to continue your revengeful assault! With rage and anger boiling in your veins, you pull the trigger multiple times with no regret or remorse!

Both, your spouse and your best-friend, have been fatally struck with multiple bullets! They both instantly die away!

A cold silence overtakes the room, as you calmly place the gun on the floor. Your boiling anger is now peacefully still. Your emotions begin to rest as your intelligence returns. You now ask yourself, "What have I done?" You now feel extreme regret, because you know what comes next. Your condition of hell will be locked-up in jail. This is what your "judgment day" brought to you. "Hell" in the form of "jail".

This occurred because, during your judgment day, you gave your decision making power over to you lower self. You gave your power to the non-thinking lower "beastly" qualities of yourself. You gave your power over to the beast in you. And the beast led you straight to hell! On a larger scale this is also what has been going on in AmeriKKKa today. We, as a Black Nation, constantly give the power of our being over to a beast, and this beast has led us straight to hell! But for now lets get back to this personal beast.

Well, what would have happened, if you would have made a different decision on that judgment day? What would have happened if you would not have given power to the beast in you? What would have happened, if you would have allowed your "higher-self" to control your lower emotions? What would have been the outcome, had you fueled your decision or judgment with "wisdom" and "intelligence", instead of "jealousy" and "anger"?

Had you empowered your higher self above your lower self, you would have avoided that condition of hell, and qualified to receive a condition of heaven instead.

Imagine the same previously mentioned dreadful situation. You step into the same situation, but this time you remain calm. Your lower emotions are quickly checked by your higher intelligence. You remain in your right mind, which is your higher states of consciousness.

So, now how do you deal with the situation? You just calmly stand there looking at them, as they scramble around trying to find their clothing. Look at them like the fools that they are. They feel totally embarrassed and even more so, because you are maintaining a calm composure.

So you just calmly walk over to your so-called spouse and say "...Well, since you are in such a hurry to find your clothing, let me assist you in finding your luggage as well, so that you will know where to put your clothing, once you find your clothing." After you calmly finish that brief conversation, you politely drive to the bank and withdraw your money from the joint bank account. Then you call the locksmith over to your house, to change all locks.

One year later, your divorce is completed, and you just met the person of your dreams! This person is so perfect for you, that you have totally forgotten your X-spouse altogether! You feel like you are in heaven! You are in heaven! This person treats you the way you have always deserved to be treated! You two live happily ever after! Heaven. No jail. No hell.

Now at the same time, your X-spouse and your X-best-friend were planning to get married, but they had to cancel. This is because they both discovered that they both were cheating on one another! They are now fighting like cats and dogs, just to discover some even more frightening news! They discovered that their extra-curricular affairs have just developed into four new cases of AIDS victims! They all angrily split up from one another, and everybody is left sick, sad, and lonely. They feel like they are in hell. They are in hell. Hell.

They all went straight to hell, because they gave their power over to that lower beast within themselves. This beast manifested itself in the form of pure lower lustful appetite! They gave this beast the power to overtake their own logical, intelligent, wisdom. This beast within, led each one of them straight to hell! The lower the beast, the lower the hell. They failed their Judgment Day. Hell is what they earned.

On the other hand, you gave your power over to the higher qualities, within your higher self. This higher self guided you to a higher condition of life! Heaven! You allowed the innate higher intelligence and wisdom to guide you through your test, trial, or judgment day. You passed your judgment day because you used the best resources in which to fuel your "judgment" or "decision". And now you ain't sweatin them fools from the past.

Once you make a habit of empowering your higher self to have dominion and rule over your lower self, you awaken your spiritual divine highest self. This highest self can lead you to levels of heaven, never before explored by the masses of the earth's population. This highest self can open new realms of existence, that you previously thought impossible. Heavens on top of heavens. The highest self is actually limit-less or infinite.

In order to achieve this level of existence, there are many trials, tribulations, tests, or judgment days that we must successfully pass. One door leads to another. Little hells lead to bigger hells and little heavens lead to bigger heavens. It is up to you. It is up to us. You can stimulate your higher self or you can stimulate your lower self. You can give your power over to the beast in you, or you can give your power over to the God in you. You can't serve two masters.

This particular subject is an important one. It has many levels of information, knowledge, wisdom, and understanding. This is enough for now. We will explore this subject more, later in our studies toward self-construction.

Peace

WHAT WOULD GOD DO?

How do we quickly return to our original mind-state? Now that our minds have been stolen away from us, what can we do to get it back?

The devil has stuck a needle in our brains. Our minds have been in the possession of the devils for centuries, and we have been made so ignorant that we willingly give our minds over to the devils. This must stop immediately, lest we receive the same doom and destruction due to the devils.

Blackmen and Blackwomen, we must save our minds, because a Black mind is the very root of our existence. And we have handed this root over to our evil enemies. Just look at our existence! We must regain possession of our own minds, or suffer the consequences. So again, how do we return ourselves to our original state of mind?

Well, there is a simple method of accomplishing this and receiving speedy results. But, in order to receive speedy results, we must be very <u>disciplined</u> in applying this simple methodology. Our goal is to completely change our whole pattern of thinking. By changing the <u>mentality</u> of a person, therefore the <u>reality</u> of a person is changed. I once heard a wise man say, "Free your mind, and your ass shall follow." Think on that.

Now, since the devil has trained and conditioned us to think like him, we want to totally cure ourselves of this fatal mental illness. We do that by attempting to achieve the opposite. We want to grow back into the mind of God.

Growing back into our original mind-state of God, is the only way to kill-off that devil mentality, that was "needled" into our brains. Growing back into the mind of God, is to accept our own and to be ourselves. The devil can not rule us, if the peace and power of God is awakened in us.

We must awaken to our true and natural selves, to destroy this evil mentality that rules us. God is "the killer" of the wicked, and God is "the life giver" to the righteous. So, growing into the mind of God, will kill off the wickedness, that is in you and controlling you, by imposing self-discipline of righteousness.

The method is simple. The method is easy. To grow into the mind of God, through self-discipline, just do this: Take every thought and action, in your life, and "critically analyze" it.

Analyze your thoughts and actions by asking one basic critical question.... "What would God do?" "Would God think this thought?" "Would God act this way?"

We should take our everyday life situations and ask, "What would God do in this particular situation?" We should take our everyday decisions and ask, "What would God decide, in this particular decision?" If we truly and honestly adopt this "simple" method, it will change our mind-states instantly and dramatically! Do you understand what I'm saying? This is the truth.

For example, think about us. Would God light up a crack-pipe? Well put the pipe down! Would God smoke a joint? Well why you gettin blunted?

Would God hang out on the corner, with a bottle of liquor in his hand, wasting time? Well, what you wasting your time for? Would God sell addictive drugs to his own people, or anybody else? Well, why you trippin like that?

Would God shoot and kill his own innocent people, for no

reason at all? So why you pointing your pistol at me? Would God put on a skin-tight, butt-huggin, mini-skirt? Well, why you dressed like a cheap ho?

Would God wear colored contacts and weaved hair in the back? Okay, so why you gotta be so fake? Would God put straightening chemicals in his hair to look like the devil? So, who is it that you are trying to look like?

Would God call the Blackwoman a "Bitch"? Well where did you learn that ignorant mentality? Would God let the devil control his future? Well, what in this hell are we doing?

Would God beg the devil to give him his equal rights? Well what you begging like a little punk for? Would God starve to death if the devil did not give God a job? What's up with us?

Would God allow his Blackwoman to be disrespected and lusted after by the devil? Well? Would God let the devil run his life? Well? Would God sit back and allow himself and his family to be oppressed, suppressed, and depressed by the devil? Well?

If the devil put God in chains, would God want to stay in hell with the devil, after getting the chains off? Well why are we still here debating over which devil to elect for president, instead of us ruling our own separate Black Nation and electing a Black god or Black goddess as our "pharaoh"?!!?

We are obviously not even close to the mind of God. We are in the mind state of a mental-slave instead of a mental master.

This mental slave shackle can be broken away, by sincerely, honestly, and continuously applying this very "simple" method, of growing into the mind of God. Make a habit of checking yourself continuously with the critical comparison to God.

If you are in opposition to God, you are automatically in support of the devil. So, make your thoughts and actions parallel to those of God. By doing this, you are being yourself. Thinking like God will solve "all" of the problems of your life, because God does not have problems. **God sees beyond problems to the solutions.** God is all knowing, all wise, all peaceful, and all powerful.

If your mind is of God, then everything else in your spiritual and physical existence will rise into place, because the mind is the root and source of "all" things. The mind is the root and source of "all" things!

The mind of the devil will bring a state of hell into your life, and those around you. The mind of God will bring a state of heaven into your life, and those around you. So, remember that if God would not do it, you should not do it. If God ain't wit it then you ain't wit it. Always ask, "What would God do?"

Peace!

WHO IS YOUR GOD?

POLYTHEISM VS. MONOTHEISM PT. 1

Who is your god? To whom do you submit your will? To whom do you give all praise? From whom do you seek all guidance? In whom do you seek all refuge? Who is your god?

This critical question is of much importance to our people. If we were to answer this question with true honesty, we would find that we are indeed and in fact a nation of "polytheists." We have a recent history of placing gods beside God.

We have a recent history of worshiping gods beside God. We always say that there is but one God, and yet at the same time we worship many "persons", "places", and "things", as gods beside the one true God. This is true. This is us. We will praise everything that God has given us, but we forget all about the merciful and beneficent God that gave us the gift in the first place. This is why we fail. Surely we are ungrateful. We are of the polytheists.

Now this subject matter applies to many aspects of our everyday lives, but as for right now, we want to focus on one segment of our "polytheism". Let us address our historical polytheism as a people, during our struggle back toward liberation. Let us examine why we fail. Let us learn from our many mistakes.

We as a people, during our struggle towards liberation, have produced many great dynamic leaders for our people. We have produced many courageous heroes, who have fought on behalf of our Black Nation for the duration of their individual lives. We have produced the most dynamic leaders in all of this world! But yet, at the same time, we still fail as a people. Well why is this? Why do we still fail?

This is because we really do not <u>follow</u> our leaders, we <u>worship</u> our leaders. We do not really <u>follow</u> our leaders, we just <u>worship</u> and praise our great leaders to death. Yes this is true.

Our people produce great leader after great leader, and all that we do is sit back and watch them do their thing. We act like we are watching a show or a performance to entertain us. We are sitting back clapping our hands and patting our leader on the back, giving up much love and praise. Well, giving honor were honor is due is a good thing, but what is an even better thing? What is an even better way of showing honor and respect to our great leaders?

Did we ever think that maybe we should "**help**" them toward their goals, instead of "**praising**" them so much? What would that leader appreciate the most, your "**help**" or your "**praise**"? Well if that leader is a <u>true leader</u>, he or she would much rather have your assistance at meeting "our" goals.

The "praise" is okay to a certain extent, but the abuse of "<u>praise</u>" don't "<u>produce</u>" nothing but inflated egos. Your "assistance" to that leader could produce a whole lot more, such as "speedy progress"!!! Are you listening to what is being said? We need to stop clapping our hands so damn much, and start using those hands and that energy to produce something other than the sounds of praise!

Your true leaders don't want you to sit down on your buttocks and just watch them do for you what you need to be doing for your own self. Why do you think that God gave us such dynamic leaders? God did not give us these great leaders for us just to sit back and marvel at them with dreamy eyes! Don't try to make God into a fool! God ain't got no time to waste on entertaining you or pumping-up some leader's ego! Hell no! God is all wise, but we have been too foolish to extract the wisdom from God's actions!

Look at us from this example of history. Let us look at the leadership of the Black Revolutionary Jesus. In case you didn't know it, that is the same Black Jesus that is written about in your dusty Bible. Not that pale-faced, hippy-haired, punk of a man that the white slave master taught you about! But anyway look at Black Jesus.

We will sit around all day shouting "Praise Jesus!!", "Jesus is my Lord and savior!!", "Praise Jesus!!!", "Jesus is my lord and savior!!!". We sound like a bunch of fools! Let me speak for myself. Jesus "**is not**" my lord and savior. Almighty God himself "**is**" my lord and savior!!! And Almighty God himself is "**your**" lord and savior too, but you are "polytheists" to the highest degree because you worship what God has given you, instead of the God that gave you the gift!

Black Jesus was, and is, a gift from God!!! He was and is a wonder-full gift from God! But he is just that, a gift! And God did not give you that gift for you to sit back and praise it, fool!!! God ain't stupid! God gave you the gift for a "<u>productive</u>" purpose! Jesus is raised to <u>teach</u> you, not to <u>entertain</u> you! The purpose of Black Jesus is to <u>teach</u> you of the knowledge of God, not to <u>entertain</u> you with the knowledge of God!!!

Give Black Jesus a break! You all up on Jesus, sweatin, spittin, and shoutin your praises to him like a fool! You just like an old foot-shufflin, bent-over, weak-minded slave! You always looking for somebody else to praise and serve like a slave! You still don't get the point!!! Do you? Why do you think that an all-intelligent God raised Jesus for us?

Black Jesus did not say to "praise" him!!! Black Jesus knows that all praise belongs to God and only God! Think about it! Jesus did not say to "praise" him, but what did Black Jesus say? Black Jesus said "follow me"! No, he did not say "praise", he said follow him!!!

But instead of following Jesus, we sit back smiling and clapping our hands, while watching Jesus as if his life is an entertainment show!!! The life of Black Jesus is not no damn show of entertainment!!! His life is a "book of knowledge!" A book of life experiences for us to use as a guide to our own life experience! His life is a compilation of teachings and guidance given to us as an example of how we should live!

God gave us Jesus as a living "instruction manual" as to how we should live our own lives! This is because we obviously do not know how to live our lives now! This is why we are so damn messed up! So, the Creator who created this life, decided to give us an instruction manual, in the form of the Black Revolutionary Master Teacher Jesus!!! You don't understand what I'm saying do you? No you don't, because you trippin off the fact that you have been so foolish for so long. But don't worry about the past! Let the dead bury their dead, and come walk on with the living.

Now since Black Jesus said to "follow" him, what does he mean by that? Jesus did not ask us to follow him because he thought that he was such a great person. Jesus did not say to follow him because he thinks of himself as being so worthy to be followed. That is a vain frame of mind!

Black Jesus said to follow him because he happened to be walking the straight and narrow righteous path. And if you followed behind Jesus, that meant that you were walking the same righteous path also.

Black Jesus did not want us just to watch him walk that walk, but he wants us to walk that same righteous path back to God. He said to come "follow" him up this path to the kingdom of the living God. He said that we were all heirs to the kingdom! To follow Jesus, meant that we would follow his righteous way of life, so that we may receive heaven just as he himself. We are to follow the God in him, that we may ultimately find and follow the God within our own selves.

But we should not just imitate Jesus to the point where we would just mock him foolishly. Not that we should wear the same brand of shoes that Black Jesus wears or that we should get our hair cut like Jesus, because those are foolish and petty things. That doesn't show God that you are down wit Black Jesus!

We are to live the basic righteous principles of life that Black Jesus lives! <u>We are to live the basic righteous principles of life that Black Jesus lives!</u> We are to take on the same type of mind state that Black Jesus has! This is what he meant by following him!!! We should take on his same values and morals of life! We should struggle, work, and labor in the name of God just like he does! We should fight against the evil devils as he does! We should do the will of God just like Black Jesus does! We should stand up and be righteous, uncompromising Blackmen and Blackwomen like God taught us to be, through the example of Black Jesus the Revolutionary!

Yes, I know that Jesus is the son of God!!! But you still need to stop jockin Jesus!!! You all up on his tip like a little parasite punk!!! Black Jesus does not live for you to praise him and jock him, fool!!! Give Black Jesus a break!!! I know that Black Jesus is the son of God! But fool, who do you think "your" father is? Ain't your spiritual father

God too? Ain't you the son or daughter of Almighty God too?

Ain't you the son or daughter of Almighty God too? Well? You always sayin "Heavenly Father." This means that you are the son of God too!!! This means that Jesus is not your "lord and savior," but Jesus is your "Black brother"! Almighty God is your lord and savior!!! Almighty God is trying to "save" you from your own foolishness through the example of the righteous Black Jesus!!! Now tell Reverend Pig-foot to go jump in his Cadillac, and drive straight to hell, with those slave-making teachings he got from his white slavemaster!!!!!

Too many times, we praise "creation" instead of praising the "Creator" that blessed us with the wonderful creation. Jesus is creation. All of our wonderful leaders and teachers are creation. So we don't fall in love with the person that brings us truth so much, that we miss the whole point; We fall in love with the truth, knowledge, and wisdom that God brings, through that person. Think on that.

You do not "praise" the delivery person so much, but you praise the one that sends you the gift through the delivery person. How many times have you received a birthday card in the mail and turned around to praise the "mail-man" for remembering your birthday? Never, because that would be foolish! You always thank the "sender" much more than you thank the "deliverer" of what is sent.

Black people stop "worshiping" your leaders as gods "beside" God. "Follow" your leader's righteous example, instead of praising them so much from the side-lines. "You" get in the game too, because we are all on God's team. But, at the same time, remember that your leader is the captain of the team and God is the owner. So don't you start no problems by always trying to be the "head nigga in charge!" You got a ego problem too, but we will discuss that later.

If you feel like you should be a leader, be patient until your turn comes. Every good leader, knows how to be a good follower first. Leave your ego, jealousy, and impatience behind. Stay unified and "follow" until you are asked to "lead". If you are real, your leadership qualities will be recognized by the people. So, let your leaders lead. Don't get in the way. Be mature. Be wise.

Let the "mind-state" of your leaders be in you. Remember that it is **"not the man"**, but **"it is the plan"**. This is the way that we can avoid failing again. Every time a leader dies, the progressive movement stops! This is because we were too busy admiring "the man", instead of learning "the plan"! This is why we go back to being the same old slave niggas, after our leaders leave us.

We become dependent upon them, like little children. If our leader dies, we should have learned enough knowledge and wisdom from God working through that leader, that we can carry on their struggle even after they leave us! We should even do a much better job, because we have the advantage of learning from the first leader's mistakes!!! Don't be a "polytheist", but be an individual in the name of God! Every time that we lost a leader, we cried like helpless babies and gave up the struggle, as if the God who gave us the first leader couldn't make another leader, even better than the first one. If we learned how to praise the Creator instead of the Creator's creation, we wouldn't cry at all. This is true, because if we really knew the merciful and beneficent God, we would better understand his wisdom.

Why give up the struggle, in hopelessness, just because our leader may have died. We should fight even harder!!! God is always alive, productive and well, if just we understand. Look at nature. Look at agriculture. Look at the apple orchard. We rejoice in the season of the harvest. This is when the tree is in bloom and the fruit is ripe and plentiful. Well after the fruit is picked and the blossoms die away, we don't cry. We don't give up in hopelessness, as if there will not be another day when the taste of sweet fruit will be plentiful again. We don't cry because we understand that the tree that produced the fruit and blossoms, is still alive. "Only" the sweet fruit and pretty blossoms have passed away, but the tree is still alive. So we don't cry.

We don't cry because we understand that harvest time will come again, as long as the tree that produced the fruit is still alive, and the fruit may be even sweeter next year, if we take good care of that tree.

Well, when our leaders pass on, don't cry. Don't cry because The Black God is The Black Tree that produces those Wonderful Black Leaders that we have had, and that we have today. And as long as we give praise and honor to that tree that produced the leader, we will reap the benefit of that tree's sweetest fruit, forever.

The day of harvest could be everyday, if we turn toward the "Creator" that the "creation" is pointing us towards. All praise and worship belongs to the One True God of Righteousness.

Accept your own responsibility, and be your own self, which is one of the sons or daughters of The Black God of Righteousness, Truth, Peace, Power, Freedom, Justice, and Equality.

"AS A MAN THINKETH, SO IS HE."

"As a man thinketh, so is he." This is a statement full of wisdom and psycho-biological science. This statement is full of concrete truth. "As a man thinketh, so is he." Let us closely examine some of the meanings of this statement. We should seek full understanding to receive the benefits of this most wise statement.

Now it is true that, "As a man thinketh, so is he." But, what does that mean? Think about that statement and its deeper meaning. This means that your thoughts, or your inward pattern of thinking, directly determines how you shall manifest outwardly. However you perceive yourself to be, this is how you will actually be. This is true, but why is it true?

The brain contains the sphere of your mind. The mind contains the sphere of your thinking. Your thinking contains the sphere of your physical and spiritual states of existence. Your physical and spiritual states of existence contain the sphere of your entire lifetime. These are spheres within spheres. The brain is the root and/or seed to your every existence.

When we were being created in the triple darkness of the Blackwoman's divine womb, our brain was the first created. And all else grew and sprouted from the brain in the same pattern that a plant grows.

All of our physical body sprouted from the seed of our brain and the stem of our spinal column. Imagine yourself upside down, physically sprouting from the root or seed of your brain. This is how we grow inside of the Black womb. Imagine a bean sprout.

Well the brain is not only the root and seed of our physical existence, but the brain is also the root of our mental and spiritual existence. The brain is a very, very, very, powerful creation. It has yet to be explored to its full capacity and potential. In today's world we use a very small minimal percentage of our brain potential.

The brain is the root of "everything". "Everything" in physical existence was formed from an idea. Every idea in existence was formed from a thought, and every thought was formed in a brain. Even the sun, moon, and stars were once just an idea or thought in a brain, but the brains of a Master-mind and not the brains of a slave-mind. Think on that. Think real good on that.

So, now that you have an idea of how all-powerful the potential of the brain is, you should understand that the brain is the master of your destiny. The brain is the master of your life's existence. Your pattern of thinking determines your pattern of life. The brain is the master computer.

The brain is your master computer. This means that however your brain or "master computer" is programmed, will directly determine the outcome of your life. If your brain or "master computer" is programmed negatively, then your life will be negative. If your brain or "master computer" is programmed positively, then your life will be positive. Do you understand what I'm saying?

For example, imagine that you have a very small one year-old child to take care of. You are in charge of developing that child's mind. You are in charge of programming that child's "master computer". So therefore you have a measure of control over that child's entire destiny of life. Right?

So how will you program that child's master computer? You could start teaching the child about science, mathematics, and the great ancestral history of our people. Then you could constantly encourage this child positively, by telling the child that he or she has great Black potential and that he or she could do anything that he or she wanted to do in life.

To constantly program this child's thinking positively towards greatness, will produce a great outcome of potential within the child. This child will think as a "mental-master" instead of a "mental-slave". This child will have Black self-confidence, Black understanding, and Black inner-security, which is the foundation of a true Blackman and a true Blackwoman.

Now, on the other hand, let us use a more familiar example of negative brain or negative mind programming. Say for example, that you take the same one year-old child under your responsibility. But this time you don't program the child's "master computer" positively, instead you program the child's "master computer" negatively.

First, you put the child in a negative environment, like the ghetto. You are raising this child in a cramped-up, small, messy apartment. You really don't pay much attention to the child, and you really don't show any affection. You only speak to the child to shout at him or her for doing something wrong. You constantly tell the child that he or she is clumsy and stupid. You always call the child a "little nappy-headed nigga". And you always saying that "a nigga ain't nothing".

In the negative environment of the ghetto, the child only sees Black people in chaos, robbing, killing and stealin from one another. When the child finally goes to school, the history teacher tells him or her that their Black historical ancestry started with slavery down in Mississippi. And that in Africa, the Black slaves were found swinging from tree to tree in the jungle, with bones in their noses, like savages.

Then you tell the child that he or she can't be whatever they want to be in this white world, because they are black. You tell them that their only real hope, could only be to land a good job working for somebody white.

Poor child, poor child, poor child. This child has just been programmed to become a "mental-slave" instead of a "mental-master". This child's "master-computer" has been programmed negatively, so therefore the child will have a negative life. The child will have a negative attitude about him or herself, and will continue to reproduce negativity in their own children generation to generation.

This child will have very low self-esteem, and this child will be a low achiever in life, because of that learned low self-esteem. This child will suffer from low self-esteem and insecurity. This child will be angry at the world! This child will have no love for themselves or anybody else!

This child is prime material for a future criminal, because what has been done to this child's mind, is criminal! It is a crime! This child's "master computer" has been programmed negatively, so therefore all that the child can hope to produce is negativity and self-perpetuated doom!!! Another mental slave!

This scenario sounds very much familiar to the way that our precious Black minds were programmed under the hand and supervision of that "Early" white slavemaster. The "Early" slavemaster had open access to our master computers, so therefore he programmed us to be slaves, niggas, bitches, hoes, sluts, and punks! He programmed us into his own image and likeness. So now that we "think" that we are nothing but a bunch of no-good niggas, we "have become" a bunch of no-good niggas. This is because "As a Black Nation thinketh, so are they!"

This slave mentality is kept alive and further encouraged or sustained by the present-day slavemasters. This present-day slavemaster has all access to our minds or "master computers" too, just like the "early" slavemaster did. This constant access is through the mastery of mind manipulative media.

Through the media, these present day slavemasters have constant access to our "conscious minds" and our "sub-conscious minds". Our minds are being wickedly led to self destruction and doom!!! The devil has literally possessed our minds and persuaded us to kill our own selves! We are putting the gun to our own heads and pulling the trigger! The devil taught us to hate ourselves, and then sold us a loaded gun! This is us! This is you! This is me! Think about it.

The mind is most important, to the healthy welfare of our being. The mind feeds every aspect of our lives with either healthy inspiration and motivation, or unhealthy depression and discouragement. The mind is a mental digestive system, that feeds your spiritual and physical existence. This brain is your mental-stomach.

So, since we now know that our minds are our "mental-stomachs", which digest whatever we mentally consume, we should be careful about the mental food that enters our precious black minds. Right? We must be carefully concerned with our "food for thought".

If we want to truly measure the quality of the mental "food for thought", we have been consuming, all we need to do is look at the true quality of our lives. Healthy "food for thought" produces a healthy mind. A healthy mind produces healthy positive thoughts and actions. Healthy positive thoughts and actions produce a healthy positive life. "You are what you eat". "You are what you eat".

So what is your "food for thought" diet? What are you mentally eating? Are you eating mental junk-food? Physical junk-food produces a weak and unhealthy body. Mental junk-food produces a weak and unhealthy mind. If your body gets sick, it is directly due to what you are physically eating or not eating. If your mind gets sick, it is directly due to what you are mentally eating or not eating. Mental illnesses include stress, depression, insecurity, low self-esteem, jealousy, ego, ignorance, confusion, fear, discouragement, etc., etc., etc.

As a Black Nation, we must really have a terrible mental diet, because we suffer from all of these mental dis-eases combined and more. We are a mentally sick people and we are plagued with mental dis-ease. Our mental dis-ease leads to our physical dis-ease, our spiritual dis-ease, and our economical dis-ease. All of this mental illness is brought upon by our mental diet or our "food for thought".

We have been allowing our historical enemies to provide our "food for thought", and yet we wonder why we are sick. Do our enemies want to see our precious Black minds at a healthy state??? Hell no, because our healthy righteous Black minds would completely destroy the wicked minds of this world, both black and white!

So, we need to start feeding our own minds with positive "food for thought". The wicked of this world want to feed you money, sex, and murder, so that you can end up a bigger fool than they already are themselves! You had better watch what you mentally eat, because it will eventually effect you directly. **We have to begin** "mentally fasting", from the consumption of what this world is serving us in the form of "<u>food for thought</u>". This is the only way to maintain mental balance, mental cleanliness, and mental health.

You can only get out of your mind, what you put into it. Your mind is already rich with mental minerals and vitamins. But they will never be utilized if you do not "farm" the mental earth. The mind is a microcosm of the earth, which is full of potential, but you have to pull that sleeping potential out, by working the ground. This is called "mental agriculture". We have to "farm" the mental earth.

You will reap what you sow. If you plant the seeds of supreme wisdom in the mind, your mind will reap the fruits of supreme wisdom. If you plant the seed one mile deep into the layers of your mind, the wisdom will come to birth and spring outward exactly one mile high, into a mountain of wisdom! You will reap whatever you sow.

If you plant the negative seeds of sex, money, murder, ignorance, materialism and fear, that the devil gave to you, do not be surprised if it springs right up in your face. You will reap what you sow. You can go either way.

Unhealthy sex seeds, will produce unhealthy lust. Misguided money seeds, will produce misguided materialism. Unjust criminal murder, will produce an unjust act of criminal murderous revenge. You will reap what you sow, from the earth and/or brain.

The potential for good and bad is contained in both the brain and the earth, it just depends on the seeds that you sow. The natural resources in the earth can be used for mass-destruction, such as nuclear technology. Or the natural resources of the earth can be used for healing the sick, such as with herbal-medicinal-technology.

So, it is the same with the mind as well. All of the potential is there. In the mind can be found the potential of mass self-destruction, or the potential for mass self- construction! The choice is ours.

As a man and woman thinketh in the core of their hearts and minds, so are they! We are what we (mentally) eat! There is no question about it! So, who is in control of your thinking? Is it you? If so, what are you doing with your freedom of control?

Who is programming your "master-computer"? Who determines the pattern of your thinking? Are you programmed as a "mental-slave", or are you programmed as a "mental-master"? Does your mental diet or "food for thought", consist of sex, money, and murder? Does your mental diet or "food for thought", consist of knowledge, wisdom, and truth? Do you mentally eat from the table of the righteous, or do you feast from the table of the wicked?

Answer these questions with sincere honesty and clarity for your own benefit. Closely monitor your pattern of thinking. Closely guard your precious Black mind from the evil access of others, and the evil of your own self. The mind is a womb, which is pregnant with a "devilish-you" or a "godly-you", depending upon whose seed was planted in this womb.

Do not intercourse with the wicked! Intercourse with the righteous, that your womb may have life and have it more abundantly! Safe-guard your heart and minds like the valuable gifts from God, that they are! Take them back from the possession of the devils! Do not allow them access to your "master-computer" anymore, lest they program you to Hell!!!

Don't think that you are a "Nigga", any longer! Think that you are an "Original Blackman" and an "Original Blackwoman"! Think that you are "The Original Black founding Fathers and founding Mothers of true civilization"! Think that you are "The Black Mental Masters of all Arts and Sciences"! Think that you are "The Black Gods and

Goddesses of the Universe"!

Think all of that because you are all of that, and then some! It is truth! Always remember that: **"As a Blackwoman and Blackman thinketh, so is he, and so is she"!!!**

Peace

GOD IS NOT WITHOUT YOU, GOD IS <u>WITHIN</u> YOU!!!

Look up... just look up and tell me what do you see! Look up! Can you see something that I can not see? What do you see? Do you see that which I can not see? Is it that I have eyes, but yet I can not see? Or is it that you have eyes, but yet you can not see?

Look up! I'm looking up too, but I don't see that which you <u>claim</u> to see. I don't think that you see what you <u>claim</u> to see either. I see clouds, skies, space, planets, sun, moon, and stars. Now what do you see? I see pyramids and a sphinx on mars. Now what do you see?

I see constellations, black holes, and other far reaching galaxies. So, now what do you see? Look up, look up and tell me what it is that I'm missing. I got 20/20 vision, so I don't think that I'm trippin.

You look up, and then <u>claim</u> to see God the "<u>Creator</u>". I look up, and say that I see the majesty of God's "<u>creation</u>". How is it that you can see what is actually not there? Are you trying to fool me into thinking that my vision is incorrect? Are you trying to deceive me, or is it just that you have deceived and fooled your own self?

I don't believe in fairytales any longer and neither should you. This world has been lying to you and me every since the day we were born, so I have learned to think for myself! I can't trust them. I can't trust the world.

They had me looking up in the sky for a fat <u>white</u> man named Santa Claus! They had me looking up in the sky for some <u>white</u> lady called the tooth-fairy! They had me looking up in the sky for some little chubby naked <u>white</u>-boy named Cupid! They had me looking up in the sky for a big <u>white</u> stork flying around with a baby in it's mouth! But most of all, they had me looking up in the sky for this hocus-pocus, invisible, <u>white</u>, spook, ghost of a God! Can you believe that? Sure you can believe it, because most of you believed it just like I did, and some of you still do!

So, wake-up! Wake-up! Wake-up! Don't live in this fantasy world of lies. The hell that you are catching everyday is "real". The devil that is giving you this hell everyday is "real".

The reason why you are catching so much hell, is because you are trying to defeat "reality" with "fantasy". Only reality can defeat reality. Stop living that lie. Don't live in childish fantasies. When I was a child, I thought and understood as a child, but now that I've matured, I've done away with childish things. Let us all do away with these childish things.

Let us all do away with this childish way of thinking that these rebellious children have imposed upon us. This childish interpretation and understanding does not belong to us, so we must do away with it. Let us now cast away our learned childish ignorance, and replace it with the ancient wisdom that is rightfully ours.

Now if you know that you have never seen anything up in the sky, other than space, then why do you continue to look up there for God? How can you put your faith and trust into someone, or something that supposedly dwells mysteriously way off in space somewhere, when you are catching all hell right here on this earth?

It sounds like you need to depend on something or someone that is a little bit closer to home. You know what they say about those long-distance relationships. "Out of sight out of mind." You don't need an "out of town" God. You need a God that is "in-sight" and "in-mind".

There ain't nothing up there for you. There is nothing up there but space. Why do you think that we call it "space"? We call it "space" because it is a geographical region that is unfulfilled by material mass. It is a region that is un-occupied, of what you are looking for! It is a region that is uninhabited, of what you are looking for! It is empty space! It is just space!

That means that there ain't nobody there! That means that don't nobody live there! Have you ever seen a sign that said "Space for Rent"? Have you ever seen a sign that said "Space for Lease"? You can't rent any space, if somebody lives there! You couldn't lease any space, if someone lives there! It is just space!

And if space was God's home, this psychotic whiteman would have flown his space shuttle up there to take it from God, just like he took everybody else's home! This crazy whiteman would have taken God's home over, and then he would have made God pay rent to stay there! And if God didn't comply with these devils, they would have tried to put God on a reservation somewhere! Can you imagine God living on a reservation making little arts and crafts to sell to tourists, or vacationing devils? You don't have to imagine too much, just take a look around you. Just look at our reality.

The evil forces of this world have fully invaded the religious world. The religious world is supposed to be the seat of righteousness during this transitory evil world. But as we know the religious world is far from that. Religion is supposed to be the direct enemy of wickedness. But, they say that the best place to find a devil, is in religion. The wicked and evil forces of this world are always seeking to <u>mis-lead</u>, <u>deceive</u>, and <u>confuse</u> those of us that are striving for truth and righteousness toward God.

They do this, because they are the direct enemies of righteousness, or of God. They would not be considered to be wicked and evil devils, if they did not do this against us. They are doing what devils are "made" to do. It is just us, that are not doing what we are "created" to do.

We are not completing our duties and objectives. The reason that we are not observant of our duties and objectives, is because we really don't <u>know</u> what they are. The reason that we really don't <u>know</u> what our duties and objectives to God are, is because we really don't <u>know</u> God. The reason that we really don't <u>know</u> God, is because we really can't <u>find</u> God. The reason that we can not <u>find</u> God, is because we are <u>looking</u> for God, in every place, <u>except</u> for where God <u>actually</u> is.

The reason that we are looking for God in the wrong place, is because we have been deceived about God, by the devil. The devil has taught us to subdue creation, instead of our Creator. The devil has led us astray from the path to God, but I don't fault the devil.

The devil is doing his job very well. I fault us! We followed the devil! We followed the devils way of thinking, even though, it didn't make any common-sense at all. The job of these evil people is to turn us away from God, while at the same time making us think that we are headed straight toward God.

These are the same people who seek to kill the prophets, messengers, and people of God. These are the same people who have historically killed you and I. They are being "themselves", but we need to wake-up and be "ourselves".

Our very present condition of life shows you that we have not found God. God is supposed to give us life and give it more abundantly. If we had found The God, we would have the blessings of life to show for it. But all that we have to show, are the abundant horrors of death, from whom it is that we have actually met.

We have not met God, we have met devil. God produces life and teaches how to produce life! Devil produces death and teaches how to produce death! So, who is it that we have been students of? Are we producing "life" or are we producing "death"?

Is this world producing "life", or is this world producing "death"??? Is this world "living", or is it quickly "dying" right before our very eyes? We have been taught to produce death. We have been taught death by death in the person. Death is what we see all around us, whether it is spiritually, mentally, economically, intellectually, or physically. Death begets death! Life begets life! We obviously have not met with "life". We obviously have not met with "God". You can tell a tree by the fruit it bares. So what type of fruit have we produced???

These points of truth should not be taken lightly, because these points are factual and indisputable! Only a fool would attempt to dispute mathematical, logical, rational, and indisputable truth. This is so plain and simple.

Of course the weak-minded persons of our community will try to desperately hold on to the madness of the past. But these words are not spoken for the foolish weak population, <u>these words are spoken for the strong, progressive, righteous populations, as a call</u>

for them to come out of this weak-world, and out of the weak people who sustain it's weakness. This is a day of separation. The strong shall progressively go on, while the weak just digressively fall further behind.

Are you of the digressive weak, or are you of the progressive strong? You must choose because the hour is very late! This is our judgment day, so I hope that we make the right judgment. The choice is totally ours.

In order for us to escape the destruction of this wicked world, we will need the active and passive wisdom of God, on our side. But, we have fully established that we do not have the aid of that wisdom now. Look at the condition of our people.

We have also established that the reason that we lack the aid of God's wisdom, is because we have been deceived about where God is to be sought after. We have allowed those persons, who have shown us nothing but mischief, murder, deception, and grief, to tell us where God is supposed to be. These people did not mentally destroy us, just to ironically turn around and show us the light of truth!

If I was a "crack addict", I wouldn't depend on a "crack dealer" to show me how to get to the rehabilitation center! That would be plain stupid of me!!! It would be stupid for the "drug-dealer" to give me accurate directions, and it would be even more stupid for me to ask my "drug dealer" to help get me off of the same "crack", that is making him rich by selling it to me everyday!!!

That's just like if we all taking a trip to heaven, but we stop and ask the devil for directions along the way! Do you really think the wicked little bastard is going to give us the correct directions? Well stop being fooled by looking up in the sky, where **h e** told you to look! The devil is so dumb that he can't even lie good, but we have been made even dumber, because we believed the shallow lies of this deceiving devil!

Okay, okay, okay! So, where is God? Since we know now where God ain't, let us find out where God is! Where is God? Where is God's home? Where is God's residing place? We must know and we must know now, that we may be reunited with the beneficent and merciful God again!!! Where is God? Where does The God live?

Did you not know that the kingdom of God was in you? Did-you-not-know-that-the-kingdom-of-God-was-and-is-in-you? Did you not know that you are the temple of the Living God? Not only is your body "A" temple, your body is "The" temple! You are the temple of the living God of life, and God's "kingdom" resides in you!

"God is not without you, God is within you!" God didn't leave you, God was with you all of the time! The problem was that you left God because you left yourself! Think about it and don't try to act confused, as if you don't understand! It is simple! Don't miss the forest for the trees!

If the "kingdom" of God-is-in-you, then where do you think the "king" lives? Stop looking up there in the sky, and answer this question! Where is the king, but in the kingdom? How are you going to find God, when you are looking for God in every place except God's home?

When you are looking for somebody, it is wise to try their home first! So, where have you been looking? You have been outside of the kingdom, looking for the King! You have been outside of yourself, looking for the kingdom! The kingdom is in you, and the king is in the kingdom, where the King should be!

We have been out here knocking on everybody's door, except for the door of the one house that we have been searching for! The house of God! The temple of God! Do you not know that ye are the temple of the Living God??? God is at the center of the universe, and wherever you are standing at any given point and time, is the center of the universe. Think about that, and think about it good!

Read your Bibles again! Don't come to me talking about what you thought Jesus said, go back and see what the precious Black Jesus said for yourself!! I'm not saying anything new, this is just what Jesus has been saying all along.

But it is hard to hear something, when you have **ears, but can not hear**! It is hard to see something, when you have **eyes, but can not see**! It is hard to realize something, when you have a **mind-set, that is not set on reality**! Leave the fantasy and come back to reality!

God is the Creator. God is our Creator. Some call God, "our Father". That would make us children of "our Father". That would make us the princes and princesses of the King! We were created in the image and likeness of our father. Children usually resemble the likeness of their parents. Children usually seek the guidance and wisdom of their parents, if that parent is righteous! Well, The God is righteous and The God is our Father!

We are the children of The God. They call Jesus the son of God. Do you not think that you are the sons and daughters of God too? Yes, you are God's children too and you are heirs to God's kingdom. The thing that makes Jesus stand out, is that Jesus is obedient to his father. That is why he is particularly beloved of The God. He has totally submitted to the wisdom and will of his father.

So, by doing this, he grew, matured, and benefited from his father's guidance. As Jesus matured, he grew from the child of his father into the same matured mind set, wisdom, and thinking of his father. Jesus became God. Jesus and his father became one in-mind and in-spirit. His mighty and wise Father taught him, so he attained to perfection.

Jesus inherited his father's kingdom. Jesus received the spiritual crown of wisdom, after he beared the material cross of ignorance. The obedience of Jesus to his father, earned for him the position of his father. His father was not going to hand over the keys to the kingdom to a fool, so he had to thoroughly test Jesus with trials and tribulations to see if he was worthy of the throne.

The righteous obedience of Jesus to God, made him worthy of the throne. Now since we are all children of God too, what do we get? Well, Jesus said that we are all joint heirs to our father's throne, but there is one catch. We have to go through our own individual tests, trials, and tribulations, just like our Black brother Jesus did. We have to earn our inheritance. The kingdom is large enough for us all.

We know that Joseph was the father of the historical Jesus' flesh (of the lineage of David), but God is the father of Jesus' spirit., and yours. We are talking about our true "Godfather". Do you understand the symbology? We are all <u>gods</u> and <u>goddesses</u>, but children of the most high God. Read Psalms. If we are growing and maturing mentally/spiritually under the guidance of our father, we don't stay children forever.

We must one day grow up into the mind of our father. God wants to give the child dominion over all there is, but that child must grow into the wisdom and intelligence of God first. We don't get the keys to the kingdom until we mature into the mind of the King. Think about that. Really think about that.

God has never been without you, God has always been within you. Right up under your nose. At your very center! At your very core! At your very root! Journey to the center of yourself! Look for the one at the center of yourself! Within you! Read Revelations!

The wisdom, guidance, intelligence, righteousness, peace

and power of God is in the person of you! It is in there, but you have to find it within yourself to make it manifest! You have to bring the kingdom of God out from within you. You must till the ground to make the earth yield harvest. God is in you! God's kingdom is in you! God's temple is in you!

Now, some of you feel uncomfortable about realizing that God is within you, because you think so low of yourselves. You deeply hate yourself due to the lies of that devil. You would hate to think that God is in you and hate to hear me say it! It makes you feel uncomfortable, so you say that it is impossible for God to be inside of anybody. You say that it is impossible for God to be in the person of somebody. You say this out of your ignorance and lack of understanding about God. You are ignorant of God because you haven't found God yet. Out of your ignorance, you believe that God is not within you, and not <u>in the person of anybody else</u>.

Are you a hypocrite? I ask you that because you can't believe that God is inside of anybody, but yet you believe that the devil can be inside of somebody. Am I telling you the truth? You believe that the devil came in the person of Adolf Hitler. You believe that people become possessed by the devil. You don't believe that God is in you, but as soon as you do something wrong, you go and say that the devil made you do it! You are a hypocrite!

You believe that the devil has the power to take over your mind, but not God? Do you mean to say, that the devil is in you, but God is not capable of being inside of you too? Well believe it or not, you are "<u>possessed</u>" by the devil in the person! You are "<u>possessed</u>" in thought, in action, in mind, in body, in spirit, in deed, and in fact!!!

The devil has you "possessed!" You have been in the devils "possession" for over four-hundred years by the devil in the person.

Your thoughts and actions are not in your "possession"! You are a slave to your master! The devil has mastered you! You are "possessed" and you are in need of an "exorcism!" You need to be freed from the illegal "possession" of the devil!

I will sprinkle this holy water of truth on you to set you free! You need free-dom (or Free-Dome)! Your head is a dome and it needs to be freed from the possession of this devil! Your mind needs to be released! Jesus said that the truth will make you free! The truth is God and God is in you! God is at the root and center of your consciousness. God is at the center of your mind!

That is why, during the crucifixion, Jesus was crowned with thorns! Thornbushes are used to keep you away! The devil wanted you to stay away from the mind-set of Black Jesus, because Black God is alive and awakened in there! The thornbush was to keep you away from the budding rose at the center! This was to keep you away from the mind-set of Jesus, which was the mind-set of God!

The biblical character of Paul told us to let the mind of Christ Jesus, be in us as well! Christ Jesus has the mind of God! The devils do not want you and I to have that mind-set, so they put a thornbush in your path! They put a crown of thorns around the head of Black Jesus, because he has a Free-Dome!

They, the devils, do not want you and I to have freedom of thought, action, mind, body, and spirit. That is why they have possessed you, and taken over your mind! They themselves, and their way of "uncivilization", are that thornbush around your head that keeps you away from the God within!

They have a shackle of thorns around your head! You are a slave to your master, the devil in the person! That is why you feel as if you have been crucified! You have been nailed to the cross and crowned with thorns! The Romans have not changed! The Roman

Empire did not fall, it just changed names to fool you! The Romans are still here giving the sons and daughters of God pure hell! The Roman-Catholic Church blessed the slave-ships that carried you off to hell! But their blessing is really a cursing! They even named the first slave ship "Jesus"!

So, they did you just like they did Back Jesus! Put you on the cross and crowned your head with thorns! They conquered and killed you in the name of Jesus Christ! The Bible in one hand and the sword in the other, with a handle shaped like a cross! The Romans ain't changed nothing but the name! God is within you and they know it! You are the devil-possessed fool, who doesn't know it! You do not know yourself, because they took your knowledge of self!

Whether you know it or not, God is not without you. You are without you. God is within you, but you are not within yourself. You are not within your original mind-state.

The Kingdom of God is within you, and you are the very temple of God. The King is in the kingdom, and that kingdom is within you. Think over that. Think over that and stay tuned for part two.

Peace

THE (NIGGA) DEVIL IN YOU VS. THE GOD IN YOU

Okay, my brothers and sisters, let us get to the point. A lot of us like to have childish fun, by calling the whiteman "The Devil", just for the fun of it. Some of us say this without the understanding of what we are really talking about.

No mentally sane, mentally healthy, Black person or any person of color, with a true knowledge of history, would deny that the whiteman is "**The** Devil". But wait a minute, because he ain't the only devil. Some of you wicked mentally-dead niggas are devils too!

Yes you can be "**A**" devil! Yes the whiteman is "**The**" devil, but some of you little wicked niggas have become "**A**" devil. Nobody has out-deviled "**The**" devil, but some of you other devils are trying to out-devil "**The**" devil! You trying to beat "**The**" devil at his own wicked game. What a shame. We need to accept our own, and be our own selves.

Well, if we need to accept our own and be ourselves, what is ourselves? Ourselves, are righteous Blackmen and Blackwomen in submission to the will of Righteousness. Well, how do we submit to the will of Righteousness? We do this by submitting to our "higher-self". Well, what is the "higher-self"? That is the nature of The God of righteousness that is innately within us at birth.

The "higher-self" is where we house and manifest the highest of our best human qualities. Now, of course, if we have a "higher-self" there must be a "lower-self". The "lower-self" is where we house and manifest the lowest of our worst human qualities.

Everything in the Universe is made from "two" basic parts. Everything in the Universe works on the law of opposites, or the law of dualities, or the law of compliments. There are two sides to everything. So, it is the same with the nature of the Blackman and the nature of the Blackwoman.

There is a stronger "higher-self" nature and there is a weaker "lower-self" nature. The stronger "higher-self" functions as the throne of God. The weaker "lower-self" functions as the throne of satan. And it is up to you, as to whom you will submit your own will to. It is up to you, as to whom you will seek for guidance.

You have two basic choices of "the God in You" vs. "the (nigga) devil in You." One can lead you into heaven-like conditions of life, while the other can lead you into hellified conditions of life. One is a peace-maker and one is a peace-breaker. You can submit your power to the God in you, or you could give power to the (nigga) beast in you. It is all up to you.

By submitting your will over to the "higher-self", your mind is being nurtured into the mind of God. By submitting your will over to the "lower-self", your mind is being nurtured into the mind of that nigga named "satan".

The mind of satan will make you do some stupid, ignorant, base-less, beast-like, evil type of things. The mind of that nigga named "satan" will provoke destructive thoughts, and therefore destructive actions.

These destructive thoughts and actions, usually turn in on themselves. Satan destroys everything including himself. Misery loves company. Even satan hates his own evil self, but he is too proud, egotistical, and arrogant, to seek righteous help and assistance to destroy his own in-grown wickedness.

This is self-perpetuated wicked self-destruction. This is the description of many of us who have this in-grown "mind of satan". We have given our power over to the beast. The beast in us. Understand that this "lower-satanic-self" is fueled, ruled, and maintained by "lustful appetite" and "petty emotions".

This is the (nigga) devil in you. This is the (nigga) devil in me. This is the (nigga) devil in us. Slay this beast on the altar. Kill this (nigga) devil in you, with no mercy! Leave it neither root nor branch.

Now, the mind of God will motivate you to manifest your highest hue-man (human) qualities. This mind state will allow you to bring out the best in yourself. Constant positive growth will be perpetuated by positive thoughts and actions.

You will not be "self-destructive"; you will be "self-constructive". This produces self-love and therefore the love of others. You truly can not love anyone else in a healthy manner, until you truly love yourself in a healthy manner. You will literally become illuminated with positive spiritual pure gleaming light!

This light will inspire and motivate others to take on the same mind of God within their own selves. This "divine-higher-self" will stand on the principles of righteousness with un-compromising strength! This mind will dominate with the ultimate peace and the ultimate power! Don't think that the mind of God is the mind of no punk!

The way that we grow in to the highest realms of the mind of

God is through strict uncompromising self-imposed discipline constantly. One must first relentlessly kill, destroy, murder, and annihilate, the wicked evil demon that lives within themselves!

No you can't sit there trying to get along with that (nigga) devil within, because it will always try to dominate you. We can not serve two masters. You must kill that bastard-beast that lives within, because that (nigga) demon will destroy you and your life!

God is all peaceful, but God is also all powerful! God is a destroyer and killer of the wicked within us and without us! Kill that "peace-breaker" and give your power of self-will over to the "peace-maker"! Let The God in you be God over you! And let the (nigga) devil in you be dead!

The mind of God will produce, intelligence, knowledge, wisdom, and truth in you! And these same qualities will fuel, rule, and maintain, the mind of God in you with divine peace and divine power!

So are you going to do the right thing now? Or are you going to keep on being the same little mentally-dead, wicked, devilish, slave-nigga, that you always been?

When you see that bottle of malt-liquor sitting on the table, who are you going to listen to? The lower (nigga) devil in you will say: "Go ahead and take a swig!" The higher God in you will say: "My brother, there is no need to alter your mind-state anymore than it is already altered. Circumstances have already reduced you to a level of ignorance and you do not need chemicals to enhance your state of ignorance." So, to whom will you submit your will?

When an outside (nigga) devil offers you a hit off a crack pipe, who are you going to listen to? The lower (nigga) devil in you will say: "Yo man, come on let's get lit off of this fool for free!" The higher God in you will say: " I already warned you once. If you follow that devil, I will multiply your addiction and allow you to send your own self straight to the hell, that you are building for your own self. Since you think that you know it all, I'm going to put it all into your hands. The choice is yours." To whom will you submit your will?

When you see another Blackman trying to do right and live right, but you ain't doing nothing right, who are you going to listen to? The lower (nigga) devil in you will say: "...look at that nigga, he think he all this and that, but he ain't bout nothing! He better not even look in my direction!" The higher God in you will say: "Look at that righteous intelligent Blackman. Don't you want to place those righteous qualities within yourself? You were not born to be a nigga, you were born to be a real Blackman!" To whom will you submit your will?

When you see a moral-less, mentally-dead, slut-like, permiscuous woman trying to offer you a fling of lustful wild sex, who are you going to listen to? The lower (nigga) devil in you will say: "Yo my nigga, you gots to get wit that! I know you gonna wax, tax, and relax that!" The higher God in you will say: "Brother you can't treat this sister like the prostitute that she is trying to be. Don't disrespect her, just because she is disrespecting herself. Sit her down and give her a knowledge of self. Tell her that she is not a 'ho' by nature! Explain to her that she is a righteous Blackwoman, who is goddess of the planet Earth and queen of the Universe by nature. But she has been made into a sex-starved, prostituting, permiscuous, cheap, ho-ish, slut, due to a circumstance of ignorance. So now that you know, stop being a ho". To whom will you submit your will?

Do the right thing for your own sake. Stop being a lower (nigga) devil, because it isn't your natural self. You learned that behavior. Accept your own and be yourself. De-throne and destroy that (nigga) devil in you. Awaken and exalt the Black God in you.

Peace

"SPIRITUAL vs. RITUAL"

Let me ask you a serious question. Let me ask you a serious question about your particular religion, or religious practices. Let me ask you a serious question about you. Are you a "spiritualistic" person, or are you a "ritualistic" person? Is your particular religion "spiritual" or is it "ritual"? What does it mean to be "spiritual"? What does it mean to be "ritual"? Is this world "spiritualistic" in its' present state, or is this world "ritualistic" in its' present state? These are very, very, very, serious questions that we need to <u>objectively</u> address, within our own personal lives.

The reason that these questions are very serious questions, is that the honest answers to these serious questions can have very serious effects on our individual lives. Notice that I used the term "honest-answers". The only way that this critical analysis can have a positive effect on our individual lives, is if we remain totally honest, during the critical analysis about our own individual lives.

Often times, we become very defensive and very emotional, when some truth is told, and when that truth just happens to hit home with us. We should not allow our personal, minimal, little, petty emotions to keep us from receiving the truth that we obviously hunger and thirst for. "Truth" is like strong medicine. It doesn't always taste good at first, but in the end, it cures the illness. So, close your eyes and open up wide, because here it comes.

There are a lot of "religious" people in this world, but there are not a lot of "spiritual" people in this world. What? What do you mean? That doesn't make sense! How can that be? I will repeat the point. There are a lot of "religious" people in this world, but there are not a lot of "spiritual" people in this world. We have been confused about these two terms, "religious" and "spiritual".

To be "religious" doesn't necessarily mean to be "spiritual" as well. This is true if we closely examine the true meanings of the two terms. There are a lot of people who are "religious" in their practices but they are not "spiritual" in their nature. Also, there are a lot of people who are "spiritual" in their nature, and are not "religious" in their practices at all. Do you understand what I am saying? Let me further explain the point.

To be "religious" is to habitually practice a particular religion. To be "religious" is to habitually practice the particular "rituals" of a particular religion. Religious practices are indeed religious "rituals".

Now this doesn't determine whether or not the religious "rituals" are good or bad, this just determines that these religious "practices", or religious "ceremonies", or religious "activities", are in fact religious "rituals". Let us try to forget, for a second, that the term "ritual" has any negative and/or primitive connotations. A ritual doesn't have to be negative or primitive, as long as it isn't used primitively or negatively.

A particular "religion" is just a particular system of particular organized rituals centered around a particular philosophy or doctrine. A "religion" is an organized system of religious rituals aimed at attaining the "spiritual". A "religion" does not automatically make you a "spiritual" person. A "religion" just provides you with a framework, network, doctrine, blue-print, plan, or system, in which you may ultimately attain "spirituality". "Religion" is merely a vehicle that one uses to get to "spirituality". "Religion" is simply a medium in which one can express his or her "spirituality" through.

We have all of these different religions but there is but one God. We have all of these different religions, but they all have the same one goal of achieving "spirituality". Well if we have the same one goal and the same one God, then what are we fighting for? God is one and the goal is one. God's people are one.

The only problem is that you have so many pure devil-hearted people who come in the name of God. These imposters seek to divide and conquer God's people, on the basis of religious titles and/or names.

All religious people want to attain spirituality, which is a high state of supreme consciousness and a high state of supreme being. In fact, I will go so far to say that all people, in general, want to attain spirituality, which is a high state of consciousness and a high sate of being. This is true. We "all" try to achieve spirituality in one way or another. For further explanation, read the chapter entitled "Gettin F'd-Up!"

You will find people everyday who are very righteous and very spiritual, but who don't necessarily practice any particular system of religious rituals. These people have found other means besides traditional religion to attain spiritual consciousness. They have found other means, in which to bring out the "best of their nature", or a higher state of consciousness and higher state of being.

These other means may be any strong positive force at work in their particular lives, to bring out the positive disciplined righteous nature and potential that is within that particular person. You find some people who are so righteous and good natured, that you just assume that they are religious people, but yet they claim no religion at all.

They attain the spiritual without the aid of any particular set of religious rituals. They are just strong spirited people by nature who are naturally righteous, and who naturally seek to do the will of righteousness. This is the true nature of Black people, if we were left alone.

These non-religious persons use and find other means of expressing their spirituality. They also find other means for stimulating spiritual growth and enlightenment. Most times, these people have found traditional religions as an "obstacle" to the spiritual realm rather than an "opening" or a doorway to the spiritual realm. Yes, there are many people who hardly ever set foot into a church, temple, synagogue, or mosque, that just literally gleam with profound spiritual light. This is true.

Now, on the other hand, there are some of us who are almost "fanatically-religious" but yet, at the same time, we possess no spiritual enlightenment at all. There are some of us who are very dedicated to the "ritual" of religion, and that is all. Even though the religious system of rituals is supposed to be systematically designed to point you toward the "spiritual", a lot of us tend to remain at just the "ritual" level.

We must remember that the outer "rituals" of religions, are just simply <u>signs</u> <u>and</u> <u>symbols</u> of different actions that occur within the inner hearts and minds of "spiritually" illuminated persons. We have become so fascinated with the <u>signs</u> <u>and</u> <u>symbols</u>, of spirituality, that we have forgotten our ultimate destination and goal. What is the sign a sign of? What is the symbol a symbol of? What is the purpose and reason behind all of these rituals? Do you remember? Did you ever know?

Well?

When I was younger, I would always have questions about religion, but I was discouraged about asking them. I was told never to question God. I didn't want to question God about anything, I just wanted to question the preacher on what he was saying about God.

God gave us inquisitive brains so that we could question and learn, but those who are ignorant of the true knowledge of God, will discourage you from questioning "them" because they are fearful that their own ignorance will show forth their inability to legitimately answer your legitimate questions. In other words, the preacher didn't know what in the hell he was talking about so he was scared to answer any questions due to his ego and his pride.

We must always remain inquisitive and curious or else we will stop growing in our knowledge. All of the different rituals and/or religions that we submit to should be thoroughly questioned. We should ask, "What is the reason or purpose behind this?" "What is the reason or purpose behind that?"

You can't receive any answers of <u>understanding</u> unless you first ask the questions of <u>non-understanding</u>. "Seek and ye shall find." Be inquisitive and be patient in receiving the answers. If your spiritual leader can not answer your questions, don't just give up right there, because he or she is not the real spiritual leader. The God is your real spiritual leader. Do not forget that. Do not ever forget that. Do not be polytheistic. You can always go straight to the source, when all else fails. For every question there is an answer. If your mind can conceive the question, your mind can eventually perceive the answer.

Your peers are students of God just like you, and some of them are much, much, much, more knowledgeable than you, but some of them are not. God is the all wise, all seeing, and all knowing.

So, who should you go to if you and your peers do not see the answers? I think that the answer is obvious. The author of truth, has truth, and is truth.

We should not allow ourselves to be constrained within the intellectual limits of our so-called spiritual leader's realm of knowledge. That leader may be very resourceful and knowledgeable, but they are still not your measure. The God is your measure, Blackman and Blackwoman, the God has no limits or limitations on knowledge, so do not limit yourself in the acquisition of knowledge and wisdom either. You are The Original People, from the immediate family of The Originator.

Use your spiritual leaders as the wonderful resources that they are, but do not totally depend on them as leaning posts. We should become dependent upon our Creator and our Creator alone.

Now, getting back to the specific subject matter, there are religious people indeed, who have gotten past the "ritual", to the ultimate goal of the "spiritual". These people practice the "religious-rituals" along with a deep understanding and knowledge of the rituals and their meanings.

These people can successfully extract the "spiritual" out of the "ritual", because they realize the purposes behind the rituals, and they realize the state of mind in which the rituals were created.

Only the knowledge and understanding behind these rituals can bring you into true spiritual enlightenment, not just merely the blind practice of religious rituals. We must always seek understanding. We shouldn't participate in activities that we don't understand or that we are not trying or growing to understand. To do that, is to literally not know what in this hell you are doing!

We don't want to be a person, who does not know what they are doing. That would be foolish. Fools do foolish things without the knowledge of what they are doing or why they are doing it. We don't want to be fools anymore.

We realize that our enemies have been fooling us for centuries, but now the joke is over because our foolishness is not a humorous thing. Although whitefolks may find "Amos n' Andy" funny, it ain't funny to most of us. We are now coming into the knowledge, wisdom, and understanding, that will crush our own foolishness and the foolishness of other fools in this foolish world!

Now, in the past, we have asked our so-called spiritual leaders for answers in the place our ignorance. They had some answers, but for most serious questions, they did not have answers.

Whenever they did not have any answers for that inquisitive person, they would say, "Don't question God." or "You don't have enough faith!" It seems that they would rather us have 90% faith in God and 10% knowledge of God. Well if the ratio is left to be that unbalanced, it is very difficult for us to put our faith into something or someone that we really don't know anything about. To say you have faith, but at the same time you have no knowledge upon which to base your professed faith, makes you a <u>subliminal hypocrite</u>. Read the chapter entitled "Faith or Blind Faith".

Okay, so let us just get down to the root of this whole "Spiritual vs. Ritual" thing. Let us just get to the point and the problem of this subject. **The problem with religions today, is that they are largely "ritualistic", but minimally "spiritualistic"**. Religions today are not producing true spiritual people. Religious heads and leaders are just simply imposing religious tradition upon their followers. People are submitting to "tradition" instead of to God. People are giving their faith over to religious "traditions" instead of God.

Why do we hold on to out-dated traditions that do nothing for us? Why do we hold on to traditions just because they are "traditional". We will never grow and expand if we keep running around in the same circles that our previous generations have also. How are we going to improve and grow like that? The purpose for history is not for us to continuously and digressively repeat it, the purpose of history is for us to learn from it and go on better equipped for the future.

So, why do we hold on to traditions that have out-lived their usefulness? Why do we hold on to religious rituals that have outlived their psychological value? Do you understand what I am saying? We continuously submit to the same traditions and same rituals that don't do a damn thing for us! Why do we carry so much unnecessary luggage?

We do this because of lack of knowledge. We hold on to the traditions of yesterday and wonder why they don't help us today. Most of these old traditions and rituals are totally irrelevant to today. The rituals and traditions of yesterday were created for yesterday, but they are still being practiced today without the "knowledge of yesterday", or the "knowledge of today."

In fact, most of these rituals and traditions are not just irrelevant, purposeless, and dead, but they are also just completely silly! Just sit back and reflect on all of the traditions and rituals that you have submitted to, and ask yourself, "Why?" Ask yourself, "What for?" Ask yourself, "What is the purpose?" Ask yourself, "Does this make any sense at all?" Be totally honest with yourself, because to lie to your own self is really foolish. If you are foolish enough to let your own self be fooled by you, then you make manifest the deepest definition of the ultimate fool!

Ask yourself these questions, and if you can not find any sensible answers, stop making a fool of yourself. It is time for our people to do away with the foolishness of the world and take on the wisdom of God. The ultimate goal is spiritual consciousness, but you can not achieve that if you are stuck in unprogressive rituals and traditions, that are weighing down your natural ascension. Cut away all of the unnecessary things that are not bringing you spiritual life.

Do away with foolishness. We can not rise spiritually if we are weighed down by the heaviness of unnecessary rituals. We must trim the fat. We must get to the root of things. At the root and at the core is the spiritual, but some of us are satisfied with the surface ritual, because the ritual does not demand much from us.

You do not have to be sincere to submit to a ritual. Anybody can submit to rituals. A devil can submit to a ritual and just fake his or her sincerity. But to attain true spirituality, one must be morally, mentally, sincerely, and spiritually correct! You have to be right to receive "spiritual" nourishment, but you can fake a "ritual" all day long!

"Little devils don't go to heaven" **Don't think that you can act a complete fool all week long and then go through a couple of rituals in your mosque, temple, church, or synagogue, to save you and make you "spiritual"!!!!!**

Some people will <u>rob, steal, kill, lie, cheat, freak, and fake</u> everyday, but yet believe that to <u>sing, sweat, spit and shout</u> on Sunday will save them from divine judgment. Well The God "judges" this type of person to be a complete fool! They know right from wrong, but to act out these religious rituals makes their conscience feel better.

If this description describes you, I have one question for you. How long are you going to continue being this fool that you are? While you are so busy trying to fool everybody else, you are the only foolish fool being fooled!!! So, stop fooling around in your foolishness fool, before you fool around and end up a permanent fool, fool!!!

Black people, it is time for us to wake-up from the foolishness of this world. Please let go of it, because it is not yours. We did not spin this web of confusion, but we are the fools that have gotten caught-up in it! All of the hypocrisy in religion is holding us back from our very spiritual nature.

You are spiritual by nature, if you are left the hell alone! You are "spiritual" in your natural essence, if you are left the hell alone! You submit to the will of God by nature, if there is no devil around to deceive you about your God!!! You are made and constructed like nature itself! Nature itself works like clockwork, if there is no devil around to distort the natural pattern of nature, by dumping chemicals, killing species of animals, or destroying rain forests!!! ...or murdering and enslaving natures' original people!!!

The native people of this land called "America", did not need any particular religion to make them a spiritual people. They are spiritual people by nature. The land was the church and the sky was the steeple. They did not need no damn tight-assed, logical-minded, left-brained, systematic, structure of rituals to keep them in a spiritual frame of mind. They were spiritually disciplined by nature! They were in constant remembrance of The God, by nature. Do you understand?

Your direct ancestors, most commonly known as the "Egyptians", were spiritual people by nature. They were spiritual people by nature, not just spiritual people on Sundays or Fridays. Their constant everyday lives were an expression of exalted divine spirituality!!! They gave spirituality, or "high spirituality", to the world! This is in the nature of The Original People. We are made like nature itself. Our construction is based on the same laws and principles.

This is our "true self", but we are now other than our "true selves".

It is only recently that spirituality had to be given "religious" names. These "religious names" were constructed by those people who are contrary to spirituality and nature itself. They had to make up names for spirituality, because it was something that they had never seen before. Spirituality was foreign and new to them. They did not live in a spiritual type of manner, up in the caves and hillsides of Europe.

So when they started being nosy and exploring (or disrupting) the civilizations of the world, they had to name this (spiritual) way of life that was so different and contrary to their own nature and way of life. They were so ignorant that they give a different name to every civilization's particular expression of spirituality, not realizing that it was actually all the same thing. This is where the division and confusion began.

Now, just to get a little deeper understanding of this big mess, let us also mention this. Our forefathers and foremothers, commonly known as the "Egyptians" (or Nubians), noticed that these folks from the caves and hillsides of Europe, were lacking in spirituality. We noticed that their thoughts and actions were contrary to mental maturity and spiritual righteousness, so we decided to help them. They were so savage, backwards, and mischievous, that we did not want them messing-up the peace of our cities and nations, so we decided to go to them where they were.

Out of the generosity of our hearts, we sent prophets, messengers, or missionaries out to teach them and minister unto them. We wanted to help them out of the savage beastlike condition that they were in. So, in order for us to do this for them, we had to be wise in our mission. Adults have to be wise in the way that they raise children into the light of understanding. This is because, if you shed too much light all at once, you can literally blind the child. So those of mental maturity must shed a little light gradually and increasingly over time until the child's mental-eye can adjust to the gleaming light of truth.

So our people are very wise and they took that knowledge into consideration. We knew that bringing these lost people into the light of spirituality would be a task, so we had to be creative in our teaching to them. Well then, our priests and priestesses devised a psychological structure of systematic rituals for these lost persons to practice.

The persons were so mischievous that we had to devise a systematic, psychological structure of disciplines, rules, and rituals, to keep them in line. We had to give them the law. We had to give them daily guidelines and systematic rituals to submit to. We had to re-train their contrary minds. This was the only way to get them to act right, by giving them strict laws, guidelines, and rituals, until they grew into spiritual maturity. We made them pray all throughout the day and night, just to remind them that there was a God of righteousness. We had to clothe them from head to toe just to keep them from submitting to their lustful nature and to keep them from rape and excessive sex amongst themselves. Strict laws and discipline was needed for these savage people. We had to teach them everything, but as you know, these people killed our missionaries, that they call prophets, and then invaded the holy lands. They then savagely destroyed the holy lands and took the holy people captive in a foreign land for four-hundred years amongst a strange people. Here we are, the seeds of our forefathers and foremothers. Read your bibles, because this history is all there. Read the walls of the pyramids because this history is all there. Take a look around you because this history is all there.

Do you now understand the value of today's religion and it's value and its purpose? Do you understand what the purpose is? Do you understand it's origination out of so-called Egypt? Do you understand that the purpose of religion is to teach and check those who are contrary to spirituality? Do you understand that? Do you understand that Black people and most people of color are spiritual by nature, if left alone? Do you understand that the traditional religious rituals of today's world are slowing down your very spiritual nature? Those religions were not created for you they were created **By** you! Buddha was a Black man! Christina was a Blackman! The Christ is and was a Blackman! Etc.!! These systems of religious rituals were created by you for other people so that they could grow into your spiritual frame of mind eventually. Do you understand that? It is so clear! These rituals were made by you but not for you!

But wait a minute Blackman and Blackwoman! You have now lost your mind totally! You are now lost! Yes, you are now lost but you can't depend upon your children and their childish rituals to show you the way to your right mind! They are now lost because they have lost your wise guidance! You have to save yourself before you save them, and they definitely can not save you! You have to be taught by God himself, back into the knowledge of who you are and what your mission and duty is to God's children! Only God in the person can help you now.

You are now the one who is lost and is living on the level of a beast. You are now the one who is childish, ignorant and mischievous and contrary to your own righteous nature. You need help now and you need some of your own medicine, but you need medicine that is <u>specifically prescribed for your nature</u>. You devised psychological medicine for others but now you need some for yourself, because that plague that came down from Europe caught everybody trippin.

Well now, since we were so merciful and beneficent enough to send missionaries with psychological medicine to the lost folks of Europe, God was merciful and beneficent enough to raise a missionary up among us for us. God gave this missionary some psychological medicine to give to us so that we might be nurtured back into our original nature. Our original nature was that of Gods and Goddesses, or what is most commonly known as angels. It is true believe it or not. The Bible says, ye are all Gods but children of the most high God. Do you understand what I am really saying? Study Egyptology.

God raised this missionary among us to minister unto us or to give us a wake-up message! Remember that we did the same thing for the other peoples of the earth, and now The God has bestowed upon us the same favor. This missionary or messenger ministered unto us for quite some time, but we obviously still didn't get the message. We most obviously still didn't get the message. We just didn't get it! Some of us thought we got the message, but most of us didn't. We are in such an ignorant state, right now, that we are reluctant to wake up to the truth.

This missionary or messenger spent his whole life trying to bring us back into our spiritual nature. But, most of us are so ignorant, right now, that we don't even realize that we are mentally, morally, and spiritually sick, so we refused to take the medicine. The truth was too strong for our taste buds. We have been mentally sick for so long that we have forgotten what being mentally healthy is all about, so we have become satisfied with being sick. Just like a sick child will close it's mouth to some medicine, we in our childish state of mind will close our ears to this missionary or messenger that comes to us.

We didn't kill or murder our messenger, but we did ignore the evil being committed against our messenger by the children of those early europeans. No we didn't kill our messenger, but we watched one of our messenger's greatest helpers be murdered. We sat back and watched the devil psychologically separate the helper from his messenger, and therefore leaving the helper outside of the protective hedge, that eventually left him unprotected from the devil. The devil divided and conquered again. The devil did not conquer the messenger, but he did conquer the helper. The devil even paid and tricked one of our dumb, stupid ignorant, sell-out asses, to pull the trigger for him. The devil will give one of us a million dollars to commit suicide, and as ignorant as we are, we would do it! We would do it, not knowing that the devil was going to take the money back after we were dead anyway! Do you know, how I know that we are stupid enough to do that? It is because our history shows that we have done it time and time again for a few pieces of silver. You just a dumb, stupid, ignorant, butt-kissing, boot-licking, brown-nosing, fiddle-playin, house nigga, sell-out!!! You and your kind are worthy of death and nothing less! If you are not a part of the solution, then you are a part of the devil-damned problem!!!

Our messenger has come and gone. We mocked, ridiculed and scorned him. We watched one of his greatest helpers be murdered right before our eyes and we turned our backs. Now lucky for us, this merciful and beneficent messenger left us with another one of his greatest helpers as a reminder to us while he is gone. At the rate we are going, God is going to take away this last helper too and leave us here to our continued doom and self-destruction.

We must wake up soon because our mischievous children are about to destroy our entire home! If you want to know who our missionary or messenger is, go get your dusty bible out. Open it to the book of Malachi and read the entire last chapter. May the peace and blessings of our merciful and beneficent Black God be upon us, because we sure need it now. The hour is late. The hour is very late.

Peace

IS IT "FAITH", OR "BLIND FAITH"?

Many religious people often ask me, what are my particular spiritual beliefs? They also ask me, what is my particular faith? I sometimes answer by saying, that "I don't function from any particular spiritual beliefs; I function from spiritual knowledge and understanding." Then I go on to say that "spiritual knowledge and understanding is the only basis upon which I can place my faith or belief."

I can not place my faith on something that I do not know of, or that I do not understand, in the least. This is just not possible for me. This should not be possible for you.

I have talked to many religious people of all particular persuasions, and I generally hear the same ideologies of "faith". We sit down together and have very stimulating intellectual conversations all of the time. I enjoy talking to religious people, because usually they are good natured people. We have a wonderful time discussing spiritual issues and different philosophies but, somewhere during the conversation, they lose me.

This is usually the part of the conversation, when they start talking about "faith" and what it is that they "believe". This baffles my mind all together. This thing about "belief" and this thing about "faith" just astounds me.

It astounds me because, just a few minutes ago, we were intellectualizing, philosophizing, and just plain using our brains to think! But all of a sudden, when it comes down to a subject upon which this particular religious person has no knowledge or understanding on, they start talking about "faith" and how you just have to "believe"!

What do they mean by saying that you just <u>have</u> to "believe"? All that I <u>have</u> to do is be righteous, stay **Black**, live, and die! I don't know where they are coming from with this particular ideology of "faith" and "belief". The conversation just stops right there.

The conversation just stops right there, because I become silent and just listen to the particular person make a fool of themselves. Like I have stated before, when I would ask different religious teachers questions, and deeply inquire about their teachings, they could not answer me. They would go on talking about how you have to just "believe" and how you just have to have "faith", and all of that childish non-sense. They told me that I should not question "God", but I told them that "I am not questioning 'God', I am questioning you!"

How can they tell me not to question things, when the book of scripture plainly says to "<u>seek and ye shall find</u>." I was just seeking in the wrong place. I was seeking the answers to my questions, but I was not finding the answers in these so-called religious teachers. The God gave me an inquisitive brain to inquire and learn about things, so I can't listen to such foolish people, or else they will make me foolish like them.

I label them as being "foolish" for one basic reason. This is because the opposite of a wise man, is a foolish one, and a wise man never ever speaks on a subject upon which he/she has no knowledge or understanding of. This is a basic rule of wisdom. A fool will try to speak on any subject, and often try to fool his own foolish self into believing that he knows what he is talking about.

When I ask religious people and religious teachers about spiritual questions that they have no knowledge or understanding about, they tend to dodge my questions, by talking about this "faith" and "believing" type of stuff. This is so foolish. When people start questioning me about spiritual questions upon which I have no knowledge or understanding, I respond by saying that "I don't know." I say that "I don't know", because I don't know! I am not going to start running-off at the mouth. I can not just run-off at the mouth about something that I have absolutely no knowledge of. That would be foolish. Right? If I don't have the answer, how can I attempt to give somebody else what I do not have myself? This is egotistical foolishness.

Some of you so-called religious teachers are not seeking "spiritual understanding" for your students, you are just seeking the "praise" of your students. So, you try to front like you know everything. Instead of directing the praise and honor to The God, you direct it straight to your false-pride and shallow-ego!

If the praise from your students makes you tall, then surely the criticism from your students will make you fall, after they wise-up to see you for who you really are. We must rise above our personal little egos.

I ask religious people to tell me their specific religious ideology. After they tell me what their ideology is, I then ask them to explain it to me. I then ask them to break it down to me into it's basic raw elements. I always become very dissatisfied, because none of my questions are usually really answered. Does this happen with you too?

I then ask the religious person to tell me what it is that they "believe". After they tell me what it is that they "believe", I say, "...now tell me what it is that you understand?" Tell me what it is that you understand about what you claim to believe. They usually try to explain, but it usually makes no sense whatsoever. It doesn't make any sense to me, and after they listen to themselves talk awhile, it makes no sense to them either.

After listening to their own foolishness, they begin to talk about "faith" and "belief". They try to put their "faith" and "belief", in the place of their lack of "knowledge" and "understanding". This is what we do sometimes. This is very convenient for us to do, during a conversation and/or debate, but it just does not cut it. So, I can not let us cheat ourselves like that. We would be doing ourselves a disservice.

So, since I can not seem to question them on their "knowledge" and "understanding", I begin to question them on their "faith" and "beliefs". I question their faith and beliefs, because I understand that they really do not have any real faith in what they claim to believe.

This is absolutely true for most religious people, when you dig deeply inside of their minds. If I were to ask them, why do they believe "this" and why do they believe "that", they would probably give me insufficient answers. They would say that this prophet said "this", and that prophet said "that". Well, I didn't ask you what the prophets said, I can read that for myself. I asked "you" why do "you" believe what "you" believe?

They would say, "I believe it because the prophets of God said so!" I would then say, "Well I'm sure that the prophets of God understood what it was that they believed in, but the question is, do you??" They would then usually become very emotional and frustrated with themselves, but vent the frustration on me.

They would then ask me, "Well brother, don't you believe in the prophets of God?" I answer them by saying, "I believe in the knowledge, wisdom, and understanding that the prophets taught, which was the wisdom of God. But, I do not place my belief and/or faith into the prophets themselves, because I am not of the polytheists. I place my faith and understanding in the wisdom of The God, that came through the vehicles and vessels of the prophets and messengers of God."

I can't go around living my life a certain way, just because somebody that I never even met before, said that I should! Please! I have to have, at least, a measure of understanding of what it is that this person is teaching before I can submit to it. I have to have "some" understanding of what I am submitting myself to! Don't just tell me what the prophets said, or what you "think" that God said, unless you are ready to explain your understanding of it! Otherwise, your mouth should be completely closed, while your ears should be completely open.

Okay, so you know what this prophet said, and what that prophet said. But can you tell me "why" they said what they said, and what did they "mean", by what they said??? Yes, you can recite what somebody else has said all day long, but until you "understand" what their words mean for yourself, you can not "benefit" from their teachings at all.

If you went to the doctor complaining about headaches, and after the examination, the doctor came out and said, *"You are suffering from the extreme over-calcification of your precious pineal glandular body, which causes a dis-harmonizing effect between your logistical and intuitive cranial brain hemispheres, that control the conscious and the unconscious activities of your cognitive perception and reasoning, that is resulting in the manifested form of painful stress produced by conflicting forces within your conscience mind, and therefore your physical body. ",* would you understand what the doctor was saying???

You could eventually memorize every word that the doctor said, but that does not mean that you would truly <u>understand</u> what that doctor was talking about! If you do not <u>understand</u> what the doctor "means", then you do not have the proper "understanding" of how to help yourself!

The doctor's diagnosis is <u>useless</u> to you, if you do not have any "knowledge" or "understanding" of the diagnosis! You don't know whether or not to pop two aspirins, or to make funeral arrangements! If you don't take the time to deeply inquire about what the doctor is saying, then you will continue to be ill. You will die for lack of knowledge.

The world has been, and still is so spiritually ill, that The God had to send us some doctors of spirituality to help us. When these prophets and messengers gave us their diagnosis of the problem, I wonder did we really understand what they really meant? I wonder this because we are still very spiritually ill! We are still very ill and it ain't the doctor's fault. They told us what was wrong, but we just did not, and do not, <u>understand</u> it for ourselves.

If we do not independently seek "knowledge" and "understanding", of our illnesses for ourselves, we then become too dependent upon the doctor's knowledge. That is why we always run to the doctor, when we get sick, because we have not <u>learned</u> how to live right in the first place! So, when that doctor leaves town, we end up right back where we started from, ignorant and ill.

We can "recite" and remember everything that the doctor said to us before the doctor left, but since we did not take the time, or mind, to truly understand what the doctor said, when the doctor said it, we therefore do not know how to heal or help ourselves while he is gone away. So, we sit around mentally ill and mentally dead, hoping, praying, believing, and having faith that someday the good doctor is going to come back. This is the absolute truth, beyond the shadow of your doubt. Do you understand what is being said?

The doctor has already completed his favor on us. We just have not completed our favor on ourselves.

All of you religious people, who claim that you have all of this "faith" in God, but yet at the same time, you really have not the least "knowledge" or "understanding" of God, are subliminal hypocrites. I do not say that to hurt you, I say that to help you see the reality of yourself, so that you can correct what is wrong and then grow-on.

You may not know it, but your claim of all of this "faith" is rather hypocritical. I say that it is hypocritical because no sane thinking human being can put his or her true faith into something of which he or she has no knowledge of. Right? Right.

You are a sane thinking person, right? I know that you are because the other aspects of your life show that to be true. You do not put your "faith" and "belief" into other aspects of your life, until you have a solid base of knowledge and understanding about that aspect of your life. Right? So, why should you do just the opposite, when it comes to the religious or the spiritual aspect of your life? If The God is not **the most** important aspect of your life, it should at least be **one of the most** important. Don't you think so?

Take this for an example. Have you ever flown on a large jet airplane before? Have you? Did you feel that it was a bit risky? Did you have to have "faith" in that flying mechanical structure, in order for you to allow it to take you thousands of feet into the air? Okay. Well, did you base your "faith" on just pure "spooky" speculation and hope??? Or, did you base your trust of "faith", on the logical and rational knowledge and understanding that millions of people have safely flown on this jet plane, many times before you??? Well?

If you did not have the mathematically rational knowledge and understanding, that people fly on jet airplanes safely everyday, would you have risked your life like that? I think not.

There were not many volunteers to fly on the first jet plane. They did not want to fly, because they did not have "faith" in it's safety. And just having a pure so-called "faith", with no knowledge nor understanding of what you are about to do, just does not suffice. The jet pilots had to make people "understand" and "know", that the jet planes were safe, before the people could put their "faith" into it. People do not usually put their "faith" into things that they don't have any knowledge or understanding of.

If I went out into the public today, and I met a very nice and intelligent sister, I am not just going to rush out and marry her. Although, I could just have "faith" that her first impression on me was a true impression, but I don't think so. "Faith" alone just obviously does not cut it, in most situations. I would have to take the time and effort to get to know this seemingly nice sister. I would have to seek some knowledge and understanding about her overall character and personality, before I could put my "faith" and trust in her. Right?

If I would not marry someone based on "faith", with no knowledge or understanding of who this person was, that would be an intelligent decision. Right? Well? Right? I would be foolish to do otherwise, wouldn't I?

I know that you would not foolishly do otherwise either, because marriage is an **important** part of life, and we don't want to mess-up! We don't want to make mistakes in our marriages, because it is **important** to us. It is close to our hearts. This aspect of our lives should be handled with care, wisdom, knowledge, and understanding. Right? Well, isn't that right? Of course that's right!

Well don't you think that your spiritual life is another **important** aspect of your life as well, that deserves your careful consideration? You will give all of that careful consideration to your "love-life", but you give your "spiritual-life" less careful consideration. You fuel your "love-life" with "faith", or trust, that is based on solid knowledge, wisdom, and understanding of who your mate is, but yet you fuel your "spiritual life" on sheer "Blind Faith" alone. Think over this.

You fuel your "spiritual relationship" on "Blind Faith", and then wonder why it ain't going nowhere! It ain't going nowhere, because you trying to fuel it with something that is not really there. That is like trying to fuel an automobile with some "make-believe" invisible gas! Don't wonder why the car ain't going nowhere!

Your "Blind Faith" is simply a veil to hide your lack of spiritual knowledge and understanding of what you claim to have "faith" in! Your "Blind Faith" is nothing but a veil that hides you from fools, but not from the eyes of the wise. You have even fooled yourself.

Wisdom is vision, and vision can see straight through your shallow veil. If you have the problem that the doctor diagnosed earlier, then you have no vision. The doctor diagnosed that your spiritual-eye was "crusty", and therefore closed. And if you do not hurry-up and wake-up, it will soon become dysfunctional.

Your veil can't hide your "choice of ignorance", from vision or wisdom. The God is the all-wise and the all-seeing. The God knows what you hide and what you manifest. So, you really ain't fooling nobody but yourself. The light of truth can shine right through your veil to show your face as it truly is! Your veil is made "sheer" through the eye of God!

Now, we have examined the other aspects of life, where

"Blind Faith" can get you into foolish trouble. We have discovered, in both examples, that "Blind Faith" can take you to a self-made doom! The only type of "faith" that you should have, is the type of "faith" that is, at least, based on some type of knowledge and wisdom of understanding.

No, **you are "not" always going to understand things immediately**. But, you should always be analyzing, intellectualizing, meditating, and contemplating on that which you do not presently understand, because this type of "prayer" (or meditation), will gradually bring you more and more understanding, in the future days.

There are going to be times when you are going to have to follow the vision of "the-wise", even when "you" may not fully understand things for yourself. But, this does not mean that you are following "blindly" or with no understanding at all. This is because you are following "the-wise", based on your resolute understanding that these wise persons are "in-fact" wise. You have come to that resolute understanding based on the historical mathematical ratio of repetitive occurrences, in which you have seen these persons, which you label as "the-wise", display their vision of wisdom. You are not going to follow a "fool", because "you are too wise" for that, yourself. Please understand this.

Now listen, if you truly understand that wicked civilizations were destroyed by The Wise God, in the past, you would also understand that this wicked world will be destroyed too! History progressively repeats itself. If you "so-call" believe that The God raised up wise "prophets" and "messengers" (*or in other words, teachers of divine wisdom*), within the midst of chaotic and confused people thousands of years ago, then surely you should be looking for a wise "prophet" or "messenger", in the midst of your own chaotic and confused people. Shouldn't you? Yes, you should, but if you are full of that "Blind Faith", your blindness will keep you from "seeing" your own wise messenger of God.

Knowledge and wisdom is vision. So, let us get some knowledge and wisdom, and begin to put it in the place of our "Blind Faith", so that we can truly see how to accept our own, and be our own **Black** selves.

Peace

THE MESSENGER CAME,

BUT DID WE GET

THE

MESSAGE???

...If you are reading this chapter, but have not read the others yet, go back and finish reading from the beginning. Stop reading, and go back. I said go back. Why are you still reading? I said stop reading! Blackfolks can really be hard-headed sometimes.

How much longer did you think that we would be left in this condition? Some people thought "forever". Some people thought that no end was in sight. That was true to a certain extent.

That was true because, there was no end in sight, according to our own "slave" vision. Our people were made "blind", deaf and dumb! So, under these severe handicaps, we could not realistically perceive any coming end to our horrible conditions, within the wilderness of North AmeriKKKa.

Now of course, if there was a <u>beginning</u> to all of this hell, there must be an <u>end</u> to it. The time was limited. Some people say, "This is just the way it is, and this is the way it's always going to be." Well, they are mistaken. Change is here. But one must have the proper "vision" to "perceive" the change that is occurring right before our eyes. This is a "great" but "dreadful" day, depending upon your level of perception.

Open your Black eyes, Black ears, Black soul, Black spirit, and Black mind, to accept your own so that you can be your Black self. We should openly receive what is being given directly to us, with all egotistical ignorance aside. All egotistical ignorance must be put aside. This is the only way to purely receive what is being given to us.

There was a remedy given to us, for our illnesses. This remedy came in the form of supreme wisdom. This supreme wisdom came in the womb of a mind. This mind came in the vessel of a man. And our salvation appeared unto us, in the form of a well made Original Man.

The Merciful and Beneficent God allowed this Black Original Man to be cured of his blindness, deafness, and dumbness. This second Adam was/is to show us that same mercy and beneficence, so that we may be cured of our illnesses also. He has worked tirelessly amongst us to deliver his message, despite his many evil enemies, both black and white. He has a message. He has a message to the Blackman. He is the messenger to us all.

I must give honor and thanks to the God, for raising one up in our midst. This one is from us, and for us. I'm speaking of The Most Honorable Elijah Muhammad. He is from and for the Lost/Found Black Nation, within the wilderness of North AmeriKKKa. He is from you and for you. He is from me and for me. He is from all of us and for all of us, and therefore he is eventually for the entire lost world, who has strayed away. But first, **we** must be saved ourselves.

I must give honor and thanks to our dearest brother, leader, teacher, and guide, The Honorable Elijah Muhammad. *I must very humbly, but proudly, profess that it is the life and light-giving teachings of The Honorable Elijah Muhammad, that inspired me, like powerful rays of pure sunlight, striking the sphere of my mind precisely at the equator, setting my previously stagnate and vestigial mind into divine rotation, making circular revolutions at a terrific speed, searching for perfect harmony with peace, power, and the flow of universal time, which is marching toward the ultimate goal of divine perfection.* Yes this is truth. Think over that.

So, why did I not mention our brother's name before now??? I did this because of you. I did this because of some of you. You know who. I did that because some of you have a "learned" prejudice against the brother. Or either your own jealousy, envy, ignorance, and reactive emotional misunderstanding, causes you to have a prejudice against the brother. Some people pre-judge without the proper knowledge of what it is that they are judging. They dispute without knowledge.

A lot of people love the truth, but just can not accept whom it is coming from. Yes this is truth! This is you. You will admit that there is truth in these writings, but if you had read this chapter first (which some of you are doing now), you might have been prejudiced. You might not have accepted the truth then. Your petty emotions might have blinded you to the truth. This is subliminal but voluntary hypocrisy maybe? I wonder.

A lot of people love the truth of the teachings from The Honorable Elijah Muhammad, but their ego, envy, and ignorance, prevents them from giving credit where credit is due. The truth is just the truth, no matter where it comes from. The truth has the same divine origination, and the same divine destination, which is the heart of the truly sincere. Yes.

So, the messenger came, but did we get the message? It

does not seem like it. But that is not the fault of the messenger; that is our own fault. We sometimes allow our lower-selves to get in the way of receiving the message. The hypocritical lower beast within ourselves, lays in the straight and righteous path, waiting to deceive then devour us. It wants to keep us from the very truth, that will ultimately give us the breath of life and give the blow of death to that beast. That lower beast must be slayed and sacrificed for the sake of higher truth.

Understand that, not only does this beast within us want to deceive us about our messenger, but so do these outer beasts. They use tricknology to confuse us and to stimulate the beast within us.

Some of these enemies will exalt, magnify, and celebrate the "**students**" of The Messenger, just to keep you from The Messenger's teachings first hand. These enemies want to keep us from becoming students of this Master Teacher too, because they fear that we may become just as dynamic as the other celebrated students.

They are afraid that, if we all go directly to the Master Teachings, we will become an entire Black Nation full of intelligent, courageous, up-right, independent Blackmen and Blackwomen! They do not want to deal with 40 to 60 million "Malcom-X" and "**Farrakhan**" (the student teacher of the hour) prototypes! I'm sure that they would not be happy with that.

They desire to keep us all as subjected, submissive, slaves, of subliminal servitude! They can not assassinate us all! We all will just bum-rush the punk that's on the trigga!!!

For those of you who read scripture, and for those of you who don't, read Bible: Genesis chapter 15, verses 12-15. Then read Malachi, chapter 4, verses 5 and 6, at the end of the Old Testament.

These scripture are talking about you, me, and us. The whole thing deals with us really. I know that whitefolks always told you that it was about them, but they lied to us again. The arch-deceiver. They have added a lot of lies to the book, but there is still of lot of truth in there. A good heart and a good mind can guide you through the symbolism, contradictions, and lies that the devil, in the person, has added to the book.

Yes, our messenger came, but we obviously have not truly gotten the message. We need to study his message and teachings, so that we may understand our place and responsibility in this world and the next world. There is an infinite abundance of wisdom within these teachings. The more your "eye" opens, the more wisdom that you can un-lock from these master teachings. You can find everything from general "Black consciousness raising", to the biological, mathematical, geographical, psychological, sociological, astronomical sciences, and then some.

The purpose of these teachings is to put us back where we belong, by giving us the proper resources to rebuild ourselves through a mental resurrection, which precedes all other resurrections. We must rise to the occasion of reintroducing civilization to the world. The purpose of The Most Honorable Elijah Muhammad's teachings is to transform us **"From Niggas to Gods!"**

Our Saviour Has Arrived with a Message To The Blackman about The Fall Of AmeriKKKa, all within The Theology Of Time. He is truly a gift to us **"A L L"!**

Peace Be Unto You!

<u>FINAL</u> <u>WORD</u> (OUTRO)

My Dearest Beloved Black Sisters and my Dearest Beloved Black Brothers, today is a good day. This is the day in which we mentally, spiritually, physically, intellectually, and morally rise "**FROM NIGGAS TO GODS**". This is so very true! If you focus the 'first eye' within your mind, you can see it too!

Our transformation is at hand! Our resurrection is at hand! Our salvation is at hand! Our time has now come again, if we would just only seize the moment!

Our only duty is to live the truth! Our only requirement is a pure heart! All that we need to do is to have the courage enough to make that first sincere step toward The God within, and the rest will naturally flow-on to take it's righteous course.

Don't worry about this devil. Worry about this God. Concentrate on this God within that is rooted in all of us. The devil is going to recklessly kill his own wicked dumb self, so don't concern yourself so much with him! As long as you are manifesting the mind, heart, wisdom, peace, power, and strength of your highest divine self, originating from The Black God within you, the devil can no longer successfully exist to commit evil!!!

We have to be about the business of re-civilizing ourselves back into full mental and moral maturity, which will cause everything else to gravitate back to it's proper place of peace.

We have many Black Master Teachers on the scene today to assist us in awakening from our ignorant slumber. I only want to inspire and motivate us to take an inquisitive interest to these beautiful Black Scholars, that we have now been blessed with Search, and find them. Read their works. Let us receive the gifts that The God has put in their hearts and minds to give to us. They want to give us what we thirst and hunger for, which is a **"Knowledge of Self"**.

PEACE

"NUFF-RESPECT"
GOES OUT TO:

THE ENTIRE ORIGINAL BLACK NATION INCLUDING, PROF. LEONARD JEFFRIES, X-CLAN, JAWANZA KUNJUFU, PUBLIC ENEMY, CHEIKH ANTA DIOP, BRO. BOB LAW, QUEEN AFUA, DR. DELBERT BLAIR, GANG STARR, BRO. WAYNE GRICE, SISTA SOULJAH, DR. KHALLID MUHAMMAD, ICE CUBE AND THE LENCH MOB, CHANCELLOR WILLIAMS III, DR. NAIM AKBAR, KRS-1 AND THE BDP CREW, DR. FRANCES CRESS WELSING, BRO. KEITH T. WRIGHT, THE JUNGLE BROTHERS, SIS. MIN. ATTY. AVA MUHAMMAD, KAM, DR. RICHARD KING, BRO. CAROL BARNES, MARCUS GARVEY, SCARFACE AND THE GETO BOYS, MASTER FARD MUHAMMAD, POOR RIGHTEOUS TEACHERS, DR. LLAILA O. AFRIKA, PROF. RONALD J. HENRY, BRO. MIN. MALCOLM X, DR. IVAN VAN SERTIMA, MASTA-ACE, THE HONORABLE BRO. MIN. LOUIS FARRAKHAN, PETE ROCK AND C.L. SMOOTH, DR. MAULANA KARENGA, BRO. KWAME TURE, ARRESTED DEVELOPMENT, DR. JEWEL PUKRAM, GEORGE G.M. JAMES, TRIBE CALLED QUEST, BRO. CLARENCE 13X, JOHN HENRIK CLARKE, TUPAC SHAKUR, THE MOST HONORABLE BRO. MESSENGER ELIJAH MUHAMMAD, DR. YOSEF BEN-JOCHANNAN, BRAND NUBIAN, DR. DONALD DOUGLAS TORY, DR. ALIM MUHAMMAD, PARIS, SIS. SUSAN TAYLOR, ETC. ETC. ETC. ETC. MUCH LOVE AND NUFF RESPECT TO YOU ALL FOR ACCEPTING YOUR OWN AND BEING YOUR BEAUTIFUL **BLACK** SELF!!!!

SPECIAL THANKS TO: SISTA MALI AND SISTA MYLENE (for your dedicated assistance), BRO. AKBAR "THE SCIENTIST" (for inspiring my brains) AND MOTHER SISTA "THE SOLDIER" (for inspiring my hearts), SISTA SHAKIRA AND BRO. HAFIZ (for sharing your much appreciated resources), AND THANKS TO SISTA ALICE AND BRO. CHUCK (for your very generous support)...

...so in other words, nuff-respect and special thanks to THE MERCIFUL AND BENEFICENT SUPREME BLACK GOD OF RIGHTEOUSNESS!!!

peace be unto us all